1993
TOTAL HOROSCOPE
AQUARIUS
JAN 20 - FEB 18

JOVE BOOKS, NEW YORK

Most Jove Books are available at special quantity discounts for bulk purchases for sales promotions, premiums, fund raising, or educational use. Special books or book excerpts can also be created to fit specific needs.

For details, write or telephone Special Markets, The Berkley Publishing Group, 200 Madison Avenue, New York, New York 10016; (212) 951-8891.

ASTROLOGICAL PERSPECTIVES BY MICHAEL LUTIN

THE PUBLISHERS REGRET THAT THEY CANNOT ANSWER INDIVIDUAL LETTERS REQUESTING PERSONAL HOROSCOPE INFORMATION

1993 TOTAL HOROSCOPE: AQUARIUS

PRINTING HISTORY
JOVE EDITION/JULY 1992

ALL RIGHTS RESERVED.

COPYRIGHT © 1977, 1978, 1979, 1980, 1981, 1982
BY GROSSET & DUNLAP, INC.
COPYRIGHT © 1983, 1984
BY CHARTER COMMUNICATIONS, INC.
COPYRIGHT © 1985, 1986
BY THE BERKLEY PUBLISHING GROUP.
COPYRIGHT © 1987, 1988, 1989, 1990, 1991, 1992
BY JOVE PUBLICATIONS, INC.
This book may not be reproduced in whole or in part, by mimeograph or any other means, without permission.
For information address: The Berkley Publishing Group, 200 Madison Avenue, New York, New York 10016.

ISBN: 0-515-10922-3

Jove Books are published by The Berkley Publishing Group, 200 Madison Avenue, New York, New York 10016. The name "JOVE" and the "J" logo are trademarks belonging to Jove Publications, Inc.

PRINTED IN THE UNITED STATES OF AMERICA

CONTENTS

MESSAGE TO AQUARIUS	5
A SNEAK PREVIEW OF THE MID-'90s	13
NOTE TO THE CUSP-BORN	15
LOVE AND RELATIONSHIPS	18
YOU AND YOUR MATE	21
YOUR PROGRESSED SUN	37
AQUARIUS BIRTHDAYS	40
CAN ASTROLOGY PREDICT THE FUTURE?	41
YOUR PLACE AMONG THE STARS	45
YOUR HOROSCOPE AND THE ZODIAC	51
THE SIGNS OF THE ZODIAC	54
The Signs and Their Key Words	67
The Elements and the Qualities of the Signs	68
The Zodiac and the Human Body	74
HOW TO APPROXIMATE YOUR RISING SIGN	75
THE HOUSES AND THEIR MEANINGS	80
THE PLANETS OF THE SOLAR SYSTEM	83
THE MOON IN ALL SIGNS	92
MOON TABLES: 1993	100
Moon Phases	105
Fishing Guide	106
Planting Guide	106
THE PLANETS AND THE SIGNS THEY RULE	107
FREE CHOICE AND VALUE OF PREDICTIONS	108
CONSTRUCT YOUR OWN HOROSCOPE CHART	113
YEARLY FORECAST: 1993	116
DAILY FORECAST: 1993	121
DAILY FORECASTS: November-December 1992	239

MESSAGE TO AQUARIUS

Dear Aquarius,

Surprises are coming, plenty of them, during this Age of Aquarius. Things are already popping in your life now. You will feel the need for freedom more powerfully than ever before. You'll have fantastic highs and lows, ups and downs, sudden changes, reversals, and scores of last-minute changes. Plans may be upset at the eleventh hour, but just when all is lost you'll get help from the place you least expect it. It's going to be a wild time. You'll be walking into situations the likes of which you've never seen before. You'll be called upon suddenly to meet challenges that will affect your future and the whole core of your ambitions. It will be a high-energy time with new risks, new dangers and new experiments. You'll stumble onto parts of yourself you never dreamed were there. You'll come upon flashes of your own genius. When it's over, you'll be a true member of the human race, for this is like an initiation phase. It will be a period of fantastic mental expansion and new awareness, and many of your childhood beliefs will be permanently transformed. Your contacts with people will make it all possible. Sound exciting? You may secretly be a little worried, though, because when things get too spontaneous and unexpected, you do get anxious and afraid.

Can predictions be possible for you—an Aquarius? They may work for a lot of people, maybe, but can accurate predictions be made for someone who always strives for independence and freedom from what *has* to

6 / MESSAGE TO AQUARIUS

happen, for the ability to live in an atmosphere of spontaneity and free choice? The answer is yes. To understand that, we have to understand you, because in a sense astrology *is* Aquarius. Astrology teaches that all twelve signs of the Zodiac are separate, individual entities existing together as a unified whole. While patterns do exist, they can and must be changed. This is largely the meaning of Aquarius.

Your higher self is the most social of all your astrological brothers and cousins. The herding instinct is deep within your nature and your great talents lie in getting all kinds of different people together in harmonious contact. You are friendly, kind-hearted, humane, you consciously strive not to harm anyone. You abhor war and violence, and are more likely than others to involve yourself with causes or movements to prevent the spread of cruelty or disease among your human fellows.

You believe deeply in the original principles upon which America was founded, although you are beyond nationality in this respect. You believe in human freedom and the right of individuals to live their lives as they see fit, in peace and harmony. You ought not dictate to others how they should live, for you cannot tolerate authoritarian conduct in others. When you feel that someone is imposing on your right to be free, you go on doing whatever you are doing, more determined than ever. You may give in to dictatorship for a while, but eventually you have to absent yourself. Although you are strong-willed and won't give in on issues of personal independence, you have an idealistic belief that it is possible for all people to live in accord without inhibitions, hangups, repressions and outworn institutions that impede progress and human development.

You believe that each man and woman has a place that he or she must find. That niche, that image or goal cannot be dictated or classified by others. It is an individual's right and necessity to go against social or cultural dictates in a conscious effort to find what is right for him or her alone, according to a wholly free and original choice. You believe that not everything is written—in law books, in the stars or anywhere. You have respect for wisdom and knowledge, but believe there are totally original moments that come out of the blue. These moments are unpredictable. You can't be tied down completely because you yourself don't know what will come in future moments, and neither does anyone else.

This is the place where we have to slow down for a moment. While you are quite right that not everything is written, the fact is that some things *are*. If you accept any standards at all, then you must accept that some things are irrevocably, undeniably, indisputably written. There are laws that may change someday, but they do exist now.

What does all this have to do with you and the predictions of this book? Simply this. The predictions are based upon planetary configurations for the next year. They are as clearly defined as the number of miles between New York and Los Angeles. As an Aquarius, you have an infinite capacity to translate instantaneously information into creative action. Predictions can foretell the quality of heavenly aspects for you, but they can never be quite sure how things are going to work out. In fact, it's often best not to try to guess exactly *how* things will end up, because once you name a possibility, it often ceases to be a possibility.

That fact is due to a planet that plays a great role in your life—Uranus, ruler of your sign. It is Uranus that will be bringing excitement during the next few years. It brings lightning changes that come flashing into our lives, brilliant streaks of insight, sudden changes of plans, things that send us on a roller coaster and release us from the dictates of our inhibitions. It is the planet of total independence, which provides the instinct for groups to form, for rebellion, and for higher intelligence to evolve.

8 / MESSAGE TO AQUARIUS

You are a child of the future, belonging to no one but yourself and mankind. You are a visionary with utopian dreams, dreaming of joy and harmony and ecstasy among people, earnestly working for the betterment of the human race. You work for funds and charities, seeking better cities and living conditions for others, or you may be involved in the great forms of media and communications, science and research, in the hopes of lifting mankind to a higher plane. Adventure is all around you, and your curiosity is an inspiration to all. It makes you fearless and courageous, restless yet tireless, in your determined effort to improve society for all its members, rich or poor.

You are humorous and open-hearted, aloof but sincere. You are like a loving visitor from another world, whose superior knowledge and advanced ideas are a source of hope and nourishment for all earthbound humans. But you remain slightly apart, as if at any moment your saucer may land and fly you away to a new world. In this sense, you are unattainable but highly desirable for your sincerity; you are loyal yet curiously detached. By remaining cool, you keep your involvements free from the passionate jealousies possible in other relationships. If your partner knows and accepts you, your relationship will be long-lasting and mutually cooperative. You often have to give up freedoms to get what you want, and this is your greatest weakness and point of self-betrayal. Your ambitions, whatever they may be, often put you in the position of having to reexamine your quest for freedom and measure it against your capacity to accept responsibility.

Everything we've been saying about you is true. In this way you are ahead of the people around you. The Age of Aquarius is supposed to represent an era of man's existence just around the corner. The astronomical origins of this term are somewhat complicated and certainly beyond the scope of this brief introduction. Briefly, it suggests a time when, spiritually and psychologically, human beings will live in peace, friendship, brotherhood and sisterhood. But before we are able to bring such a golden age into reality, how can we free ourselves of our narrow-minded intolerance and the bigotry of our existing conventions and institutions? If we throw out *all* the rules and start over, we might be making a drastic mistake.

Nobody is completely free from inhibitions, responsibilities, feelings of inadequacy, needs or dependence. If you lived without any rules or duties, your life would have no structure or method. Without a definition of purpose, there could be no accomplishment, your dreams could never be realized. The application of discipline to genius will not impede success but assure it.

That is why you are such a valuable member of the Zodiac. The machinery of the law is interminably slow, and society does not like to change once it is comfortable with a given reality. Then you come along and —zing!—the picture changes. You, too, have private inhibitions, the desire for honor, prestige and acceptance, inner needs to be free from scandal or reproach and well-equipped with a share of prejudice against prejudice. You have to learn to be as tolerant of custom and authorities as you are of rebels and minorities. You may live your life within the Establishment, but you have the zeal of a revolutionary within you. You've been born with a talent for giving people the notion that your thing is the right thing whatever it is. But when you meet strong views that threaten your own, how tolerant are you?

The question of discipline and freedom annoys you, and you often have inconsistent behavior patterns when it is put to the test. Responsibilities weigh heavily on you; you resent any restrictions on your desire to do exactly as you please. You prefer to design new worlds, but building them requires time, effort, patience and self-control, which you aren't so willing to give. You suffer from guilt about your responsibilities, and you can switch from liberalism to conservatism almost without warning.

In your romantic relationship you need an ardent lover with a strong, passionate ego, someone who has a strong sense of self, who can let you do your thing without making demands. You need a central force and direction toward which you can focus your allegiance. Your intellect is brilliant, shining and often liberated from background and schooling. You were born intelligent, with a magical curiosity. You are a dynamo of brain power. But you often lack centrality of purpose. Although you are a pleasant, cooperative individual, you sometimes lack a spark of enjoyment that other people can provide. You find the truth spread throughout many people, and it is hard for you to focus on one person for an indefinite time. Your loyalty, on the other hand, is deep and sincere. Only a fascinating and strong figure could capture you for a long time, and only if you were granted freedom and separation.

You're happiest when your lifestyle is a departure from the usual. You're apart from humanity in this way and often go out of your way, quite naturally, to live and dress in a fashion that sets you apart from people with the obsession to dress and live and talk alike. Maybe you can't figure out why you do some of the things you do. But you're not malicious or bitter; you're a person who honestly needs to act the way he feels. You're naturally a truth-seeker, who is traveling the road toward justice. You may be an Aquarius who lives a "regular" life for years and years, dressing and acting like everybody else, but you will not be able to continue this forever. Total social conformity would poison your whole system. Your life needs a unique element.

In all areas of your life, work and relationships, you have spurts of energy, interest and curiosity. Your best work and loving are done during these intense spurts. This is why a nine-to-five job is harder for your freedom-loving nature. You will probably be lucky and find a livelihood you can devote yourself to, away from other people's rules and regulations. You might end up working longer hours than you would with a regular job, but you will enjoy finding your own rhythm. Of course, there are moments when even the freest artist requires extreme self-control and discipline. You have the power to consciously channel energy, if you will develop it.

Your financial worries are often a combination of real and imagined fears. Money slips through your fingers and you may find yourself being "taken" at times. Your genuine feeling for the needs of others makes it hard for you to refuse help to those in need. You're most secure when you are working, but you also need change and independence. If your work fluctuates, so does your income. But you believe in taking chances and living at the edge of the runway, ready for takeoff and a new experience. But your roots are often more money-oriented than you care to admit. Though your aims are humanistic, money and possessions are some of your deepest involvements. That is a source of perplexity you can rarely escape.

There's a side of you that enjoys being a little weird, pulling out of situations at the last minute to express your independence. You can be a disruptive force in someone's life and you enjoy seeing plans upset and changed because of you. You will cause scandals in your sphere through brazen breaches of accepted standards of behavior. This wild exuberance, which crashes through every social barrier, is both charming and disarming. But you can be thoughtless of other people, or perhaps not so much thoughtless as coolly uncaring, especially if your ethics or personal standards are involved. When you think you are right you get caught up in a spirit of rebellion. Your whole life can meet upheavals so that you'll often be doing something totally new, something you are totally unprepared for, yet you will succeed at it.

12 / MESSAGE TO AQUARIUS

The challenge of the surprise situation is the food of your soul. It reaffirms one of your basic principles: you can't plan everything. Some things just have to come into a situation at the last minute. You can throw a room together, pin your clothes on as your guests arrive, and come off smashing. Of course, everything may not be as solid as it looks, but it will have a flair and style that will be totally acceptable in some crazy way. You like futuristic surroundings with antiques sprinkled here and there.

You are the Water-Bearer of the Zodiac, pouring the water of life and intelligence for humanity to drink. You are the arteries and veins of the cosmic body. On Earth your own body is ruled by the circulatory system, lower legs and ankles. Problems are often worked out through the arteries and veins and by reflex action to the heart and spine, throat and sex organs; usual stomach adjustments have to be made. Your physical well-being depends on your mental outlook and your capacity for interchange with people.

At some point you must break away from the expectations and patterns set for you by others, and find your own road to freedom. Try to be a good friend.

Michael Lutin

A SNEAK PREVIEW OF THE MID-'90s

In this last decade of the twentieth century, planetary aspects for the mid-'90s give you a hint of what is to come. Major changes already begun will continue, and some will be completed in 1995 and 1996. The years ahead afford great opportunity for meeting challenges, discovering hidden paths, and achieving new strengths.

Aquarius individuals, ruled by Uranus and Saturn, will gain in prestige as lofty aims are tapped. For the past several years and through 1995, Pluto in Scorpio is affecting your house of career and worldly ambitions. Your attitudes toward fame and fortune are changing as you seek to make your mark. Although professional advancement and high community standing are goals, you are not destined for a solitary life. Close relationships are necessary and desirable.

With Jupiter in Libra most of 1993 your affectional life is in a state of flux. Your airy sociability invites new alliances, which vie with long-established ones. While Jupiter is in Scorpio November 10, 1993 through December 8, 1994, you have no qualms about discarding certain ties in order to focus exclusively on one love partner. A hopeful, happy, lucky period for intimate relations coincides with Jupiter's transit of Sagittarius December 9, 1994 to January 2, 1996. By leading the family, in matters of both business and children, your informed idealism lights the way.

Uranus and Saturn take center stage in creating dramatic change for Aquarius. Uranus sparks your genius, Saturn builds self-discipline. When radical thought is sobered by reasoned judgment, the result is tremendous productivity. Your output encompasses the personal and the political, the artistic and the commercial, so you earn emotional satisfaction and financial gain. Uranus is in earthy Capricorn till early 1996. Then Uranus enters your sign January 12, 1996 for a seven-year residence. With Uranus in Aquarius, you're on! You can achieve notable recognition for inspired output.

Saturn in Aquarius till early 1994 is an honorable placement, promoting intellectual growth through service to the community. Saturn in Pisces January 28, 1994 to April 6, 1996 fortifies your humanitarian interests, while inspiring your artistic expression. The insights you gain from Saturn in Pisces deepen your sensitivity to people and strengthen your commitment to them. Pisces' ruler Neptune, the planet of mystery and vision, is in Capricorn through 1999. Your belief in social reform must be backed up by thoughtful action so you do not waste your visions in fits and starts. Jupiter in Capricorn almost all of 1996 helps by sharpening your organizational skills. When the big ideas come into focus, you can order your priorities and through perseverance achieve them one by one.

New aspects from fire signs starting in 1995 and 1996 fuel the Aquarius heart and mind. Pluto begins a long transit of Sagittarius on November 11, 1995. Pluto in Sagittarius into the next century kindles your reforming zeal, as it affects your house of community ideals, hopes, goals, and friendships. Saturn enters Aries on April 7, 1996, and the road ahead twists and turns with surprise challenges. Saturn in Aries gives you an unwavering sense of duty but poses conflict between solitary ambition and community participation. With Uranus in Aquarius, your ruler in your sign, you cannot stray too far or too long from the ones you love. You are the architect of a rich collective life.

NOTE TO THE CUSP-BORN

Are you *really* an Aquarius? If your birthday falls during the fourth week of January, at the beginning of Aquarius, will you still retain the traits of Capricorn, the sign of the Zodiac before Aquarius? What if you were born later, in February—are you more Pisces than Aquarius? Many people born at the edge, or cusp, of a sign, have difficulty determining exactly what sign they are. If you are one of these people, here's how you can figure it out, once and for all.

Consult the table on page 17. It will tell you the precise days on which the Sun entered and left your sign for the year of your birth. If you were born at the beginning or end of Aquarius, yours is a lifetime reflecting a process of subtle transformation. Your life on Earth will symbolize a significant change in consciousness, for you are either about to enter a whole new way of living or are leaving one behind.

If you were born around the last two weeks of January, you want to be free. You're committed somewhere because you want to be, not because some heavy figure stands behind you pulling the strings. You may want to read the horoscope book for Capricorn as well as Aquarius, for Capricorn holds the keys to many of your hidden uncertainties, secret guilts, subtle motivations and all your cosmic unfoldment from an occult point of view.

You are a person who will always break free from

limitations or obstacles, or you will break your leg trying.

When it comes to discipline you are ambiguous and complex. You need discipline to survive and succeed, but you openly reject it. Inwardly you find it hard to escape from the old problems of total freedom versus strict routine and structure.

You have a grain of the conservative in you, a bit of the authority figure and a thirst for power you can't seem to shake. But peace is your mission and friendliness is your purpose.

If you were born the third week of February you are either a mad genius or you are just avoiding jail by the skin of your teeth. You may want to read the horoscope book for Pisces as well as Aquarius, for through Pisces you tap your talents and convert your assets into profits for others as well as yourself.

Your great love is ad-libbing, for there is no thrill like pulling something off at the last minute and *succeeding*. Your great successes come from last-minute reversals, unexpected turns of fate and the famous cavalry coming charging over the hill. You have the touch of the prophet—utopia with a touch of doomsday thrown in. When you are at your best you are being a friend.

DATES SUN ENTERS AQUARIUS
(LEAVES CAPRICORN)

January 20 every year from 1900 to 2000, except for the following:

January 19:		January 21:		
1977	1989	1903	1920	1932
81	93	04	24	36
85	97	08	28	44
		12		

DATES SUN LEAVES AQUARIUS
(ENTERS PISCES)

February 19 every year from 1900 to 2000, except for the following:

February 18:				February 20:
1900	1954	1973	1989	1917
21	57	74	90	
25	58	77	91	
29	61	78	93	
33	62	81	94	
37	65	82	95	
41	66	85	97	
45	69	86	98	
49	70	87	99	
53				

LOVE AND RELATIONSHIPS

No matter who you are, what you do in life, or where your planets are positioned, you still need to be loved, and to feel love for other human beings. Human relationships are founded on many things: infatuation, passion, sex, guilt, friendship, and a variety of other complex motivations, frequently called love.

Relationships often start out full of hope and joy, the participants sure of themselves and sure of each other's love, and then end up more like a pair of gladiators than lovers. When we are disillusioned, bitter, and wounded, we tend to blame the other person for difficulties that were actually present long before we ever met. Without seeing clearly into our own natures we will be quite likely to repeat our mistakes the next time love comes our way.

Enter Astrology.

It is not always easy to accept, but knowledge of ourselves can improve our chances for personal happiness. It is not just by predicting when some loving person will walk into our lives, but by helping us come to grips with our failures and reinforce our successes.

Astrology won't solve all our problems. The escapist will ultimately have to come to terms with the real world around him. The hard-bitten materialist will eventually acknowledge the eternal rhythms of the infinite beyond which he can see or hear. Astrology does not merely explain away emotion. It helps us unify the head with the heart so that we can become whole individuals. It helps us define what it is we are searching for, so we can recognize it when we find it.

Major planets have been operating on the sign of Libra and have changed people's ideas about love and commitment. Since Libra is the sign of marriage, partnerships, and relationships, these factors have affected virtually everyone in areas of personal involvement. These forces point out upheavals and transformations occurring in all of society. The concept of marriage is being totally reexamined. Exactly what the changes will ultimately bring no one can tell. It is usually difficult to determine which direction society will take. One thing is certain: no man is an island. If the rituals and pomp of wedding ceremonies must be revised, then it will happen.

Social rules are being revised. Old outworn institutions are indeed crumbling. But relationships will not die. People are putting less stress on permanence and false feelings of security. The emphasis now shifts toward the union of two loving souls. Honesty, equality, and mutual cooperation are the goals in modern marriage. When these begin to break down, the marriage is in jeopardy. Surely there must be a balance between selfish separatism and prematurely giving up.

There is no doubt that Astrology can establish the degree of compatibility between two human beings. Two people can share a common horizon in life but have quite different habits or basic interests. Two others might have many basic characteristics in common while needing to approach their goals from vastly dissimilar points of view. Astrology describes compatibility based on these assumptions.

It compares and contrasts through the fundamental characteristics that draw two people together. Although they could be at odds on many basic levels, two people could find themselves drawn together again and again. Sometimes it seems that we keep being attracted to the same type of individuals. We might ask ourselves if we have learned anything form our past mistakes.

The answer is that there are qualities in people that we require and thus seek out time and time again. To solve that mystery in ourselves is to solve much of the dilemma of love, and help ourselves determine if we are approaching a wholesome situation or a potentially destructive one.

We are living in a very curious age with respect to marriage and relationships. We can easily observe the shifting social attitudes concerning the whole institution of marriage. People are seeking everywhere for answers to their own inner needs. In truth, all astrological combinations can achieve compatibility. But many relationships seem doomed before they get off the ground. Astrologically there can be too great a difference between the goals, aspirations, and personal outlook of the people involved. Analysis of both horoscopes must and will indicate enough major planetary factors to keep the two individuals together. Call it what you will: determination, patience, understanding, love—whatever it may be, two people have the capacity to achieve a state of fulfillment together. We all have different needs and desires. When it comes to choosing a mate, you really have to know yourself. If you know the truth about what you are really looking for, it will make it easier to find. Astrology is a useful, almost essential, tool to that end.

YOU AND YOUR MATE

AQUARIUS—ARIES

You may meet out of nowhere and strike up a full-blown friendship. It may develop into a high-plane, long-lasting relationship of support and mutual understanding, which makes valuable contributions to each of your lives. A partnership that is successful for you both might seem strange to the people around you, for you are a volatile blend of independence and bohemianism. You may try to make your life simple, free from traditional jealousies and cloying attachments, and in that way you could make the relationship work. You need innovation, change, excitement and the element of *what next?* Variety will keep fanning the flame of this match as long as it lasts.

When the newness wears off, you could fall out of each other's lives as fast as you fell in. When jealousy and possessiveness replace a free and easy style of living and respect for each other's way, sudden and violent flareups will occur. Explosive confrontations will threaten the peace and can cause irreparable damage to a growing and fruitful friendship. Involvements are getting more powerful now, and new emotional, sexual scenes may be tipping the scales. Experimentalism and self-will can bring separations to this relationship. But greater growth is possible through this exciting and high-energy time.

Hints for Your Aries Mate:

There are endless possibilities in the union of Aquarius and Aries. The strength of both your personalities will come in handy when you fight to save the relationship, which you will be doing a lot of. Keep the affair from being shortlived by proving that you are as adventuresome as Aries. Plan an overnight camping trip together or go to Europe for six months on $2000. Trouble may brew when you discover that Aries expects you to play a traditional sexual role. This expectation will go against your radical grain. But if you play along with the role for awhile, Aries will lose interest in maintaining it, and then you will be free to go back to your liberated ways. At about this time, you will want to go off the deep end about the flirting habits of your mate. Before you jump, remember that Aries' superficial interest in a few other people is a jealous response to your deep interest in all peoples of the world. Allowing Aries this small freedom will cement the relationship.

AQUARIUS—TAURUS

You are a marriage of money and nonconformity. Together you can present an image of wealth, careless elegance and a gracious bohemian style. As a pair you can be stable and eccentric, practical and zany, well ordered or horribly disarrayed. It will be war, at times, between an earthy pragmatism and an impulsive spontaneity. The conflict will take place between a private sense of financial need—a primarily self-seeking desire for gain—and a more detached, less personal and highly humanitarian need to act freely out of human friendship—in short, a conflict between personal duties and human freedom.

At worst, you will bring out all the weapons of greed and disruption in each other. At best, your combined spirit will be loyal and practical, so that you are both freed to explore your individual freedoms. Sexually you can be a fruitful team, combining rugged physicality with unusual experimentalism—providing one of you doesn't get too fearful or withdrawn.

Utilize your creative potential together through new opportunities, reversals, changes, and sudden turns of fate.

Hints for Your Taurus Mate:

If you are serious about this relationship, be prepared to give in a lot. Then you will be the beneficiary of the Taurus ability to nurture, smooth over, and make everything right with the world. Fighting your partner's need to set the tone of what you do together will only make you seem the naughty child. Giving in to this need will have a calming effect on your manic personality. When the demands become too much, you can always escape to your world of fervent causes. Since Taurus is very happy relating to the home, she or he will not resent being left to domestic devices. On the other hand, when the demands of your public life overwhelm and drain you, you won't find a more nourishing lover than Taurus. Know that you can come together in your love of the performing arts. Make up for the war between your personalities by frequently taking your lover to the theatre and to concerts. Spending money on your partner is one of the fastest ways to the Taurus heart.

AQUARIUS—GEMINI

Aquarius can love Gemini with an adoring selfless devotion, and yet the relationship may never get down to Earth, or stay there long enough to provide any traditional kind of security. The attractions are powerful.

24 / YOU AND YOUR MATE

You are both alike—you need your freedom, and commitment is difficult. You both know from experience that tomorrow will bring its own surprises, no matter what promises you make today.

Your cosmic paths have crossed. The blending of your souls, minds or bodies may be harmonious, sweet, unimaginably high. But if you both do not have adequate outlets to refresh yourselves and regenerate through other people, your magic flower will wilt quickly. The powerful electricity that zaps you when you are together will turn off—permanently.

Together you can be a humorous pair, enjoying each other's youthful rebelliousness and appreciation for the absurdity of many social rules. You can flout conventions and laugh at what people expect from you, but you may ultimately lack permanence, purpose or support of each other. Share your interest in people.

Hints for Your Gemini Mate:

The danger in this relationship lies in the similarities. You love your independence, but so does Gemini. In spite of your dreaminess, you'll be the one to hold the union together. Your partner wants to be in charge, but Gemini is not always as sensible as he or she likes to think. You may find yourself cleaning up the mess from the dinner party Gemini presides over. Compensation will take the form of wit, energy, and creative lovemaking, qualities that abound in Gemini and that you value in a lover. After Gemini talks you into believing that she or he can't live without you, the flirtation period sets in. Don't panic or feel betrayed. This is merely Gemini's way of maintaining his or her individuality, something you are quite capable of doing yourself. Your partner loves to be wooed with gifts and praise, and will return the compliments tenfold. If you cannot afford separate living quarters, then be sure you have a room with a door that locks.

AQUARIUS—CANCER

Why would two people like you ever get together? Cancer is supposed to need a stable, peaceful atmosphere. You are supposed to live for the moment, spontaneously and without traditional ties. Actually, as foreign to each other as you are, you are the link between the old and the new. If you can reconcile these basic differences within yourselves, you make something valuable out of knowing each other.

Each of you can bring out the erratic, negative qualities of the other. Childish, vain and disruptive, you can battle each other on levels of chaos and emotionalism, playing on maternal and paternal needs, shattering each other's yearning for tenderness and closeness, pulling the rug out from under each other, clinging and fleeing in an endless cycle of attachment followed by separation or aloofness.

At best, you join in your desire for security and adventure. You could design a whole new way of living, one that respects the need for human attachments and honors the traditions of the past but makes significant breakthroughs at the same time, freeing you both from all your past conditioning and neuroses. In some unconventional way you could live for yourselves, independently, in the present, and still not shatter your desires for peace, tranquility and happiness. It is not a usual type of union.

Hints for Your Cancer Mate:

The self-indulgence of your Cancer mate may get on your nerves. Your ability to think on a world scale will be directly opposed to your mate's desire to dwell on a spot on the wall. If you can think of your partner as a practitioner of your theory, then you will appreciate his or her nourishing, humane qualities. The tug will be felt most when Cancer wants to hide under the bed and you want to lead the Fourth of July parade. Take your mate's shy qualities seriously. If Cancer won't go to a community meeting or a discotheque, then suggest a movie or a quiet, romantic restaurant where you both know the waitress. In other words, start small if you hope to coax Cancer out of the social or political closet. Assure your partner that she or he needn't be Perle Mesta in order to keep your love. The special attention you pay to Cancer's need for peace and security will be returned in the form of fierce loyalty and the key to your soul.

AQUARIUS—LEO

You are perfect opposites. You join the qualities of a hot-blooded lover and the detachment of a scientist. Where one of you is well-ordered and dignified, needing stability, planning and control, the other is disarrayed and ultracasual, craving spontaneity and unpredictability. Where one of you demands attention and obedience, the other is wandering and rebellious.

But you complete each other perfectly, and you can symbolize the utter union and reconciliation of two opposing personalities. As long as you recognize each other's separateness, you can be joined. You need to accept the fact that many of your partner's traits are part of you, too. Then you can welcome each other into your lives.

At worst, you can bring out cruelty and selfish domination or perverse, upsetting irresponsibility in each other. The more one gets possessive and bossy, the further detached the partner becomes. The more one demands allegiance, the less support the other is able to give.

At best, you are the blend of a warm heart and an intelligent mind. You can reflect the joys of a deep private love and the human need for people, associations, and friendships outside the realms of usual love affairs.

Hints for Your Leo Mate:

You'll be making a mistake if you think that Leo's brassy personality has nothing in common with yours. Chances are that this is the person you've been seeking to give yourself an excuse to get swept away. Leo's big-time approach to everyday problems may cause you to feel like an armchair liberal. Try not to get depressed when your partner comes straight to a point that you've been pussyfooting around for months. Realize that there is room for both viewpoints, and don't get sucked into competing with your partner. She or he does not like to come out second best, so you'll be in for the fight of your life. In the whirl that surrounds Leo, you are likely to forget that you have qualities, such as intelligence and imagination, to which Leo is very attracted. Since you both enjoy the atmosphere away from home, you'll find togetherness in socializing. Your outside interests will give Leo a chance to wear those snazzy clothes which take up so much room in your closet.

AQUARIUS-VIRGO

You are a curious blend of vibrations. Both highly intelligent beings, you are interested in each other but unfortunately have only a limited capacity to grasp each other's realities. You are sincere, peace-loving people with an earnest desire to help your fellow man. You can be coolly detached, dedicated scientists, both devoted to your separate lives and separate work, but still finding each other highly exciting and humane creatures. You respect each other's intelligence and admire the capacity of one to focus on specifics and the other to develop a wide spectrum of talents.

At worst, you can resent each other for your own undeveloped traits. It can be a war between order and disarray, propriety and disruption, manipulative control and personal freedom. Together you can be petty and calculating, unsupportive and unpredictable. Where your partner needs purpose, you can get picky and faultfinding. Where your partner needs emotional breadth, you can be cool, separative and noncommittal. You might start by playing the roles of policeman and juvenile delinquent or you might cover your mistrust under the masks of hard-working enthusiast and irresponsible rebel.

At best, yours is a deep and lasting friendship, weathering separations and basic life differences. You are joined in the mind, and capable of ingenious offspring, for you blend the powers of cool reason and personal genius.

Hints for Your Virgo Mate:

Your belief in free love will clash with Virgo's belief in monogamy. Just remember that neither of you is likely to practice what you preach. So let that argument pass when it comes up. What you won't be able to bypass is your mate's criticism, which will be right on the nose in regard to you. Virgo likes to make dents in your armoring. If you are clever enough, and you are, to turn the tables on him or her, you'll learn to control your mate's critical attacks. Pointing out Virgo's shortcomings will send your mate scampering for defense mechanisms, which are never far away. Learn to let your partner save face by turning to solitude. Virgo's need to be alone is not a retaliation for your criticisms, but rather a chance to restore identity, away from your harsh judgments. If you learn to respect the Virgo desire for mystery, you will have a mate for life, one who will eternally intrigue you.

AQUARIUS—LIBRA

If you want a partnership with strong, healthy roots, this can be it. But don't forget that with you comes the one element Libra didn't bargain for. Libra will not be able to tolerate flagrant disruption long. Emotional insecurity or perverse rebelliousness will damage the union. You cannot allow perpetual domination forever. If your freedom is too stringently curtailed, separation is usually the ultimate choice. As a team, however, you come equipped with a unique blend of patience, a capacity to bend, and a certain elasticity when it comes to solving problems that pop up unexpectedly. There is a good humor, a cool, level-headed detached approach that can allay fears, bring enjoyment and weather the sudden storms that can come up out of nowhere.

You can be friends and companions, lovers, or husband and wife, but your relationship willl have a strange twist, an unusual set of conditions under which it will grow. You can have a turbulent on again—off again romance. You may war between romance and detachment, emotional drama and cool reason, marriage and freedom, but at best you are a friendly pair of lovers. You need maturity, honesty and the sense of duty and responsibility to succeed in this union.

Hints for Your Libra Mate:

In this relationship you have met your match in ability to dispute with brilliance. If you allow yourself to be carried away by your Libra partner, you will find your feet planted more firmly on the ground. Don't be frightened by the Libra ability to clarify. It is not going to reduce your strong beliefs in a more egalitarian world. Prove your intellectual security by engaging your partner in frequent philosophical discussion. He or she will be sexually turned on by your desire to test your intellectual strength. Encourage your mate's socially adept side by giving dinner parties to which you invite a variety of types and classes. Create a setting for the expansive and graceful talents of Libra. Give Libra room to breathe, and she or he is yours for life. The pitfall you must avoid is the desire to sit by the hearth. Your Libra's hearth is so enticing, but later you may accuse your mate of tricking you into staying away from political gatherings.

AQUARIUS—SCORPIO

Diplomacy, right conduct, love of justice, and even separation are key solutions to the problems between attachment and freedom. If such conflicts threaten to shatter your dreams of peace, nevertheless they will bring you both to a new and exciting understanding of yourselves as individuals and in relation to each other. You are both looking for security and yet may find it hard to make serious total and long-lasting commitments. You cannot simply let go and let yourselves be free, yet you fear each other when you dig in and get possessive.

Your conflicts are between the intimate one-to-one relationships of your forefathers and the free-style open scenes of experimental relationships. You struggle between needing deep sexual involvement and open nonsexual relationships with friends in a spirit of community, fellowship and harmony. Your relationship can vary from tenderness, intense concern, and mutual growth and nourishment, to abrupt coldness and separation—and a peculiar lack of tenderness and feeling.

You can have a long-lasting relationship provided

you don't get bossy or just leave your partner hanging to show your independence. Some rules are made to be broken. Mature individuals who love each other naturally receive the respect and concern of their partners.

Hints for Your Scorpio Mate:

Your chief reaction to this intense and passionate organism may be terror. Scorpio will not be flattered by such a reaction, so shake it by daring to stand your ground during one of his or her privately pitched battles. The stormy temperament of your Scorpio mate is something to admire, not escape. Learn to see through the syle. It is not so much the content that is diametrically opposed to yours as it is the form. Show that you trust Scorpio's morality and vision by inviting your mate to a political meeting or demonstration. Most likely you will get a refusal, since Scorpio is more interested in saving a stray lamb than a whole flock. Although Scorpio is constantly testing your reaction to her or his outrageous behavior, you will not feel alone in your attempt to hold the relationship together. When you most need it, you will sense your partner's drive and determination to make you feel loved. If anyone can erode your refined exterior, Scorpio can.

AQUARIUS—SAGITTARIUS

Together you could write a new Declaration of Independence, for you both abhor domination and restrictions. You are both dreamers, idealists at heart. You share an honest desire to live happily and in peace, doing exactly as you please. You both fight commitment, and thus your friendship should either be totally casual and spontaneous or set up with a definite structure that is agreeable to both parties.

You can both flout rules and amuse or abuse each other with your pranks and mischief. Even when caught being naughty, you understand each other, for you are both incorrigible and lovable. In the name of freedom, you could adopt a course of disruption and wanton rebellion.

Yet you are the intelligent members of the human race, the learned humanitarians whose love of people, truth, knowledge and enjoyment ultimately must light the way for others. You believe that people should live in freedom and peace. When the laws and structures of society interfere with that individual liberty, you will take action. You will risk and gamble everything for what you believe in.

Together you can be the symbols of evolved intelligence, and with a little help from your more practical friends, you'll be able to realize your ingenious schemes, inventions, plans and dreams. Arrange this friendship in an unconventional way. Freedom is all.

Hints for Your Sagittarius Mate:

In your determination to give Sagittarius the freedom you both believe in, you may overshoot your mark. Keep your mate from drifting away by accompanying her or him, now and then, to a basketball game or to an ice skating rink. Sagittarius is easy to make happy, so easy that you may overlook the possibilities. Since it takes so much to win you over, it will be hard to believe that you can make your mate beam with a pat on the head. The jock veneer could make you flippant about Sagittarius' intellectual side. If you manage to rope him or her into one of your political meetings, you'll be surprised at your partner's political savvy. You'll also be surprised at his or her vehemence about winning an argument. Help your partner to develop an esthetic sense by popping into a museum or art gallery while you are both out for a vigorous walk. But don't proselytize.

Follow the Sagittarius example of live and let live, and you'll have fun.

AQUARIUS—AQUARIUS

You are both peace-loving spirits. You believe in living and letting live, and yours could be a lifelong and fruitful friendship. You are both seeking the happy union and fellowship with other human beings, in which you can live in freedom and joy. For you two, the Age of Aquarius has already started.

At worst, anarchy and disruption could characterize your lives. There could be an aimlessness to your lives, a perfectly harmonious situation of freedom, but a freedom with nothing to do. Your lives could lack conflict and confrontation, and you could be strangers at the end.

At some point in your association, there will be a strange twist that affects you both profoundly, something unlooked for and totally unexpected that changes your perspective and puts you in a different place. You will receive a jolt that will effect a powerful transformation over your life. Through death, or sex, or the sudden entrance into your lives of a new person, or some bolt-from-the-blue, your lives will change drastically.

Hints for Your Aquarius Mate:

It may just be that you have met your true love. The possibilities of the relationship will strike you as limitless. All the soaring that both of you tend to do will make it hard to come down to earth. Raving about how lucky you both are will be the highlight of most of your conversations. It will be up to somebody to ground you lovebirds, and it may as well be you. Make a point of participating in activities other than meetings, lectures, or symposiums. Organize a physical fitness program for the two of you. If you can't stand jogging, take up biking or day-long hikes. That way you can integrate your needs by walking and talking at the same time. And don't forget about sex. You may have to schedule this activity. The creative lovemaking abilities of Aquarius could be wasted if you don't force your mate, and yourself too, to take some action. Don't get into the habit of doing without sensual pleasure. It could turn out to be the high point of your union.

AQUARIUS—CAPRICORN

You're an interesting pair because you can be very close while still being so deeply different. Together, both of you feel the need to be shy and reserved and yet long to be explosively spontaneous. Neither of you enjoys being bombed out of your reserved self, but you don't like your desires curtailed by any controlling forces. Capricorn and Aquarius together can be torn between rigid discipline and chaotic disruption, caught by conflicts between your ambitions and your sense of independence. Each of you must accept and respect the other's need for privacy, independence, and security. For this relationship to develop properly, you must hold on to your Aquarius freedom and give Capricorn your support in return. You both desire liberation from life's limiting routines, and method is your greatest tool to that end. The relationship is complex, to say the least.

At best, you are the union of reason and genius, the symbol of the orderly transition from the old to the new.

Hints for Your Capricorn Mate:

The trick in this relationship lies in keeping your head above water. Since you tend to control the hedonistic side of your nature, Capricorn's lavish approach could sink you if you aren't on guard. But give in to your mate's desire to organize, and you could find yourself succeeding where you used to fail. Irritation will be your first response to Capricorn's sycophantic but essentially naive reaction to the famous and the fortunate. Help your mate to see through the glitter by not overreacting to his or her impressionableness. This characteristic is merely a cover for lack of confidence. To help build that confidence, take your partner to the next movie preview you are invited to. Make a big point of introducing him or her to your famous friends. Capricorn functions well when there is a frame or structure to the proceedings. You'll find mystery in the relationship if you look for the glamorous soul beneath the accountant's exterior.

AQUARIUS—PISCES

You will probably have a long and fruitful friendship, once you have passed through your major battle. Your conflict is between freedom and bondage, and your relationship may well surpass the understanding of everyone around you. There is the deep spirit of fellowship, plus a sincere feeling of compassion and forgiveness, but it will have its element of subtle gameplaying, guilt and control. Pisces will be responsible for the total reassessment of Aquarius values. What seems external and permanent one day will slip away and vanish the next.

Pisces will try to escape from you time and again, but you are linked in a cosmic cycle from which there is no escape. The delicacy of your relationship depends on many subtle factors. You have a need for risk, danger and the company of people, coupled with the desire for secrecy, intimacy and emotional security. You can go on self-indulgent kicks, experiment with this pleasure and that, then find yourselves off on an unconventional spiritual mission. The chaos and lack of continuity to your lives could be followed by a sudden reversal and conversion to conservatism and home-style living. You are both lovers of change and experience—and there is your strong point.

Hints for Your Pisces Mate:

This relationship will be hard to grab hold of. But if you try, you'll be making a mistake. For the most part, your job will consist of creating a protective environment for your Pisces partner. If you want to take him or her to a social or political event, you'd better go ahead and stake out a safe corner for your shy, self-doubting flower. With a Pisces partner, you are liable to behave in an even more unconventional manner than usual. Your mate will admire you for being untraditional and daring, and will vehemently defend your right to be so. But don't let this you're-all-right attitude fool you. Pisces has high intellectual and moral standards, and will tell you when you don't come up to them. This will be attractive to you. From time to time you will need to escape from this emotionally draining personality. You can trust Pisces to enjoy the solitude that results from your departure. If you enjoy hard work, this is the relationship for you.

YOUR PROGRESSED SUN

WHAT IS YOUR NEW SIGN?

Your birth Sign, or Sun Sign, is the central core of your whole personality. It symbolizes everything you try to do and be. It is your main streak, your major source of power, vitality and life. But as you live you learn, and as you learn you progress. The element in your horoscope that measures your progress is called the Progressed Sun. It is the symbol of your growth on Earth, and represents new threads that run through your life. The Progressed Sun measures big changes, turning points and major decisions. It will often describe the path you are taking toward the fulfillment of your desires.

Below you will find brief descriptions of the Progressed Sun. According to the table on page 39, find out about your Progressed Sun and see how and where you fit into the cosmic scheme. Each period lasts about 30 years, so watch and see how dramatic these changes turn out to be.

If Your Sun Is Progressing Into—

PISCES, a spiritual need for reconciling failure with success is necessary now. Guilt, disappointment, and sorrow are illusions that must be pierced, for beyond them lies redemption. If you are plagued by doubts, anxieties or uncertainties, be assured that success and happiness will come through devotion, faith, compassion, forgiveness, and love.

38 / YOUR PROGRESSED SUN

ARIES, you start gathering a sense of who you are, a basic zest and enthusiasm for life. You speak up for yourself and become more open and honest. You'll feel more aggressive and will respond to challenges more readily. You may even *look* for challenge. You will experience an awakening to your self.

TAURUS, you begin to acquire possessions and wake up to your earthly needs. Money enters your life in a significant way. Though your fantasies grow richer, you need to develop your earthly sense of values. You want to earn your own way and be paid for your efforts.

HOW TO USE THE TABLE

Look for your birthday in the following table; then under the appropriate column, find out approximately when your Progressed Sun will lead you to a new sign. From that point on, for 30 years, the thread of your life will run through that sign. Read the definitions on the preceding pages and see exactly how that life thread will develop.

For example, if your birthday is January 30, your Progressed Sun will enter Pisces around your 21st birthday and will travel through Pisces until you are 51 years old. Your Progressed Sun will then move into Aries. Reading the definitions of Pisces and Aries will tell you *much* about your major involvements and interests during those years.

AQUARIUS / 39

YOUR PROGRESSED SUN

If your birth-day falls:	start looking at PISCES at age	start looking at ARIES at age	start looking at TAURUS at age
January 20-21	30	60	90
22	29	59	89
23	28	58	88
24	27	57	87
25	26	56	86
26	25	55	85
27	24	54	84
28	23	53	83
29	22	52	82
30	21	51	81
31	20	50	80
February 1	19	49	79
2	18	48	78
3	17	47	77
4	16	46	76
5	15	45	75
6	14	44	74
7	13	43	73
8	12	42	72
9	11	41	71
10	10	40	70
11	9	39	69
12	8	38	68
13	7	37	67
14	6	36	66
15	5	35	65
16	4	34	64
17	3	33	63
18	2	32	62
19	1	31	61

AQUARIUS BIRTHDAYS

January 20	Federico Fellini, Patricia Neal
January 21	Paul Scofield, Jack Nicklaus
January 22	Lord Byron, D. W. Griffith
January 23	Stendhal, Manet, Jeanne Moreau
January 24	Edith Wharton, Maria Tallchief
January 25	Somerset Maugham, Virginia Woolf
January 26	Paul Newman, Eartha Kitt
January 27	Wolfgang A. Mozart, Lewis Carroll
January 28	Arthur Rubenstein, Colette
January 29	William McKinley, Germaine Greer
January 30	F. D. Roosevelt, Vanessa Redgrave
January 31	Tallulah Bankhead, Carol Channing
February 1	Clark Gable
February 2	James Joyce, Stan Getz, Ayn Rand
February 3	Gertrude Stein, Joey Bishop
February 4	Lindbergh, Ida Lupino, Betty Friedan
February 5	Belle Starr, Red Buttons
February 6	Ronald Reagan, Zsa Zsa Gabor
February 6	Charles Dickens, Buster Crabbe
February 8	Lana Turner, Jack Lemmon
February 9	Gypsy Rose Lee, Amy Lowell
February 10	Jimmy Durante, Leontyne Price
February 11	Thomas Edison, Kim Stanley
February 12	Abe Lincoln, Charles Darwin
February 13	Kim Novak, Bess Truman, Patty Berg
February 14	Galileo, Jack Benny, Thelma Ritter
February 15	Susan B. Anthony, Claire Bloom
February 16	Sonny Bono, Katherine Cornell
February 17	Marian Anderson, Margaret Truman
February 18	Jack Palance, Helen Gurley Brown
February 19	Copernicus, "Mama Cass Elliott"

CAN ASTROLOGY PREDICT THE FUTURE?

Can Astrology really peer into the future? By studying the planets and the stars is it possible to look years ahead and make predictions for our lives? How can we draw the line between ignorant superstition and cosmic mystery? We live in a very civilized world, to be sure. We consider ourselves modern, enlightened individuals. Yet few of us can resist the temptation to take a peek at the future when we think it's possible. Why? What is the basis of such universal curiosity?

The answer is simple. Astrology works, and you don't have to be a magician to find that out. We certainly can't prove astrology simply by taking a look at the astonishing number of people who believe in it, but such figures do make us wonder what lies behind such widespread popularity. The United States alone has more than ten million followers, and in Europe there are 25 million or more. Everywhere in the world hundreds of thousands of serious, intelligent people are charting, studying, and interpreting the positions of the planets and stars every day. Newspaper columns and magazine articles appear daily, broadcasting brief astrological bulletins to millions of curious readers. In Eastern countries, the source of many wisdoms handed down to us from antiquity, Astrology still has a vital place. Why? Surrounded as we are by sophisticated scientific method, how does Astrology, with all its bizarre symbolism and mysterious meaning, survive so magnificently? The answer remains the same. It works.

42 / CAN ASTROLOGY PREDICT THE FUTURE?

Nobody knows exactly where astrological knowledge came from. We have references to it dating back to the dawn of human history. Wherever there was a stirring of human consciousness, man began to observe the natural cycles and rhythms that sustained his life. The diversity of human behavior must have been evident even to the first students of consciousness. Yet the basic similarity between members of the human family must have always joined them in the search for some common source, some greater point of origin somehow linked to the heavenly bodies ruling man's whole sense of life and time. The ancient world of Mesopotamia, Chaldea, and Egypt was a highly developed center of astronomical observation and astrological interpretation of heavenly phenomena and their resultant effects on human life.

Amid the seeming chaos of a mysterious unknown universe, man has from earliest times sought to classify, define, and organize the world to which he belongs. Order: that's what the human mind has always striven to maintain in an unceasing battle with its natural counterpart, chaos, or entropy. Men build cities, countries, and empires, subjugating nature to a point of near defeat, and then . . . civilization collapses, empires fall and cities crumble. Nature reclaims the wilderness in the midst of man's monuments to himself and society. Shelly's poem *Ozymandias* is a hymn to the battle between order and chaos. The narrator tells us about a statue, broken, shattered and half-sunk somewhere in the middle of a distant desert. The inscription reads: "Look on my works, ye mighty, and despair." And then we are told: "Nothing beside remains. Round the decay of that colossal wreck, boundless and bare, the lone and level sands stretch far away."

Man has always feared the entropy that seemed to lurk in nature. So he found permanence and constancy in the regular movements of the Sun, Moon and planets and in the positions of the stars. Traditions sprang up from observations of the seasons and crops. Rela-

CAN ASTROLOGY PREDICT THE FUTURE? / 43

tionships were noted between phenomena in nature and the configurations of the heavenly bodies. This "synchronicity," as it was later called by Carl Jung, extended to thought, mood and behavior, and as such developed the astrological archetypes handed down to us today.

Astrology, a regal science of the stars in the old days, was made available to the king, who was informed of impending events in the heavens, translated of course to their earthly meanings by trusted astrologers. True, astrological knowledge in its infant stages was rudimentary and beset with many superstitions and false premises. But those same dangers exist today in any investigation of occult or mystical subjects. In the East, reverence for Astrology is part of religion. Astrologer-astronomers have held respected positions in government and have taken part in advisory councils on many momentous issues. The duties of the court astrologer, whose office was one of the most important in the land, were clearly defined, as early records show.

Here in our sleek Western world, Astrology glimmers on, perhaps more brilliantly than ever. With all of our technological wonders and complex urbanized environments, we look to Astrology even now to cut through artificiality, dehumanization, and all the materialism of contemporary life, while we gather precious information that helps us live in that material world. Astrology helps us restore balance and get in step with our own rhythms and the rhythms of nature.

The contribution of Astrology to twentieth-century life is more vital than ever. Each new advance in scientific knowledge increases the skill and know-how of our great age. Yet each confirms and develops ancient astrological principles at the same time.

It is usually wise to be a little skeptical and not accept other people's ideas too quickly without thought or examination. Intelligent investigation of Astrology (or the practical application of it) need not mean blind acceptance. We only need to see it working, see our own lives confirming its principles every day, in order to accept and understand it more. To understand ourselves is to know ourselves and to know all. This book can help you to do that—to understand yourself and through understanding develop your own resources and potentials as a rich human being.

YOUR PLACE AMONG THE STARS

Humanity finds itself at the center of a vast personal universe that extends infinitely outward in all directions. In that sense each is a kind of star radiating, as our Sun does, to all bodies everywhere. These vibrations, whether loving, helpful or destructive, extend outward and generate a kind of "atmosphere" in which woman and man move. The way we relate to everything around us—our joy or our sorrow—becomes a living part of us. Our loved ones and our enemies become the objects of our projected radiations, for better or worse. Our bodies and faces reflect thoughts and emotions much the way light from the Sun reflects the massive reactions occurring deep within its interior. This "light" reaches all who enter its sphere of influence.

All the stars in the sky are sending out vast amounts of energy and light. Their powerful emissions affect every other body everywhere in space. The more science uncovers, the more astonished we become at the complex relationships of all things in the observable universe. Everything is in constant motion and change, yet somehow caught in a gripping attraction almost too awesome to comprehend.

Recent investigations have now uncovered new sources of energy, powerful emitters of different kinds of radiation, such as radio galaxies, pulsars and quasars. These may be almost unimaginably distant bodies, smaller perhaps than a single star, yet brighter than a whole galaxy. Black holes, too, are a recent and mysterious discovery—pockets of dark areas in outer space, perhaps holes in the fabric of our universe through which we might someday travel to other universes. Preposterous? Not at all. Such remote forces could be more strongly linked to us here on Earth than most of us would ever care to think.

Our own personal radiations are just as potent in their own way, really. The reactions that go on deep within us profoundly affect our way of thinking and acting. Our feelings of joy or satisfaction, frustration or anger, must eventually find an outlet. Otherwise we experience the psychological or physiological repercussions of repression. If we can't have a good cry, tell someone our troubles or express love, we soon feel very bad indeed.

As far as our physical selves are concerned, many of us fail to see the direct living relationship between our outer lives, inner reactions and actions, and the effects on our physical body. We all know the feeling of being startled by the sudden ring of a telephone, or the simple frustration of missing a bus. In fact, our minds and bodies are constantly reacting to outside forces. At the same time we, too, are generating actions that will cause a reaction in someone else. You may suddenly decide to phone a friend. If you are a bus driver you might speed along on your way and leave behind an angry would-be passenger. Whatever the case, mind and body are in close communication and they both reflect each other's condition. If you don't believe it, next time you're really angry take a good long look in the mirror!

In terms of human evolution, our ability to understand, control and ultimately change ourselves will naturally affect all of our outside relationships. Astrology is invaluable to helping us comprehend our inner selves. It is a useful tool in helping us retain our integrity, while cooperating with and living in a world full of other human beings.

Let's go back to our original question for a moment. Why is it that even the most wary among us still has a grain of impressionability when it comes to hearing about the future? Everyone would like to part the mysterious veil and see what lies beyond. But even if it is possible to do so, what good can it do us to look years ahead? To know that fully, we must come to an understanding of what the future is.

In simplest terms the future is the natural next step to the present, just as the present is a natural progression from the past. Although our minds can move from one to the other, there is a thread of continuity between past, present and future that joins them together in a coherent sequence. If you are reading this book at this moment, it is the result of a real conscious choice you made in the recent past. That is, you chose to find out what was on these pages, picked up the book and opened it. Because of this choice you may know yourself better in the future. It's as simple as that.

If we could keep our minds clear and free from worry, anxiety and unrealistic wishes, it should be quite possible to predict events and make conclusions about the "synchronicity" of heavenly events and their earthly manifestations. By being totally aware of the present with all its subtle ramifications and clues, the future would be revealed to us with astounding clarity. Knowing ourselves is the key to being able to predict and understand our own future. To learn from past experiences, choices and actions is to fully grasp the present. Coming to grips with the present is to be master of the future.

"Know thyself" is a motto that takes us back to the philosophers of ancient Greece. Mystery religions and cults of initiation throughout the ancient world, schools of mystical discipline, yoga and mental expansion have always been guardians of this one sacred phrase. Know thyself. Of course, that's easy to say. But how do you go about it when there are so many conflicts in our lives and different parts of our personalities? How do we know when we are really "being ourselves" and not merely being influenced by the things we read or see on television, or by the people around us? How can we differentiate the various parts of our character and still remain whole?

There are many methods of classifying human beings into types. Body shapes, muscular types, blood types and genetic types are only a few. Glandular, racial and ethnic divisions can also be observed. Psychology has its own ways of classifying human beings according to their behavior. Some of the most brilliant contributions in this field have been made by Carl Jung, whose profound insight owed much to his knowledge and understanding of astrological processes.

Other disciplines, too, approach the study of human beings from different points of view. Anthropology studies human evolution as the body-mind response to environment. Biology watches physical development and adaptations in body structure. These fields provide valuable information about human beings and the ways they survive, grow and change in their search for their place in eternity. Yet these are all still "branches of science." Until now they have been separate and fragmented. Their contribution has been to provide theories and data, yes, but no lasting solutions to the human problems that have existed since the first two creatures realized they had two separate identities.

It's often difficult to classify yourself according to these different schemes. It's not easy to be objective about yourself. Some things are hard to face; others are hard to see. The different perspectives afforded to us by studying the human organism from all these different disciplines may seem contradictory when they are all really trying to integrate humankind into the whole of the cosmic scheme.

Maybe with the help of Astrology these fields will unite to seek a broader and deeper approach to universal human issues. Astrology's point of view is vast. It transcends racial, ethnic, genetic, environmental and even historical criteria, yet somehow includes them all. Astrology embraces the totality of human experience, then sets about to examine the relationships that are created within that experience.

We don't simply say, "The planets cause this or that." Rather than merely isolating cause or effect, Astrology has unified the ideas of cause and effect. Concepts like past, present and future merge and become, as we shall see a little later on, like stepping-stones across the great stream of Mind. Observations of people and the environment have developed the astrological principles of planetary "influence," but it must be remembered that if there is actual influence, it is mutual. As the planets influence us, so we influence them, for we are forever joined to all past and future motion of the heavenly bodies. This is the foundation of Astrology as it has been built up over the centuries.

ORDER VS. CHAOS

But is it all written in the stars? Is it destined that empires should thrive and flourish, kings reign, lovers love, and then . . . decay, ruin and natural disintegration hold sway? Have we anything to do with determining the cycles of order and chaos? The art of the true astrologer depends on his ability to uncover new information, place it upon the grid of data already collected, and then interpret what he sees as accurate probability in human existence. There may be a paradox here. If we can predict that birds will fly south, could we not, with enough time and samples for observation, determine their ultimate fate when they arrive in the south?

The paradox is that there is no paradox at all. Order and chaos exist together simultaneously in one observable universe. At some remote point in time and space the Earth was formed, and for one reason or another, life appeared here. Whether the appearance of life on planets is a usual phenomenon or an unrepeated accident we can only speculate at this moment. But our Earth and all living things upon its surface conform to certain laws of physical materiality that our observations have led us to write down and contemplate. All creatures, from the one-celled amoeba to a man hurrying home at rush hour, have some basic traits in common. Life in its organization goes from the simple to the complex with a perfection and order that is both awesome and inspiring. If there were no order to our physical world, an apple could turn into a worm and cows could be butterflies.

But the world is an integrated whole, unified with every other part of creation. When nature does take an unexpected turn, we call that a mutation. This is the exciting card in the program of living experience that tells us not everything is written at all. Spontaneity is real. Change is real. Freedom from the expected norm is real. We have seen in nature that only those mutations that can adapt to changes in their environment and continue reproducing themselves will survive. But possibilities are open for sudden transformation, and that keeps the whole world growing.

YOUR HOROSCOPE AND THE ZODIAC

It's possible that in your own body, as you read this passage, there exist atoms as old as time itself. That's right. You could well be the proud possessor of some carbon and hydrogen (two necessary elements in the development of life) that came into being in the heart of a star billions and billions of years ago. That star could have exploded and cast its matter far into space. This matter could have formed another star, and then another, until finally our Sun was born. From the Sun's fiery mass came the material that later formed the planets—and maybe some of that primeval carbon or hydrogen. That material could have become part of the Earth, part of an early ocean, even early life. These same atoms could well have been carried down to the present day, to this very moment as you read this book. It's really quite possible. You can see how everything is linked to everything else in a most literal way. Of course, we don't know exactly when or how or why the Earth was created. But we do know that it *was* created, and now exists in a gigantic universe that showers it constantly with rays and invisible particles. There is no place we could go on Earth to escape this very real, albeit invisible, cosmic bombardment. You are the point into which all these energies and influences have been focused. You are the prism through which all the light of outer space is being refracted. You are literally a reflection of all the planets and stars.

Your horoscope is a picture of the sky at the moment

of your birth. It's like a gigantic snapshot of the positions of the planets and stars, taken from Earth. Of course the planets never stop moving around the Sun even for the briefest moment, and you represent that motion as it was occurring at the exact hour of your birth at the precise location on the Earth where you were born.

When an astrologer is going to read your chart, he or she asks you for the month, day and year of your birth. She also needs the exact time and place. With this information he sets about consulting various charts and tables in his calculation of the specific positions of the Sun, Moon and stars, relative to your birthplace when you came to Earth. Then he or she locates them by means of the Zodiac.

The Zodiac is a division of the Sun's apparent path into twelve equal divisions, or *signs*. What we are actually dividing up is the Earth's path around the Sun. But from our point of view here on Earth, it seems as if the Sun is making a great circle around our planet in the sky, so we say it's the Sun's apparent path. This twelvefold division, the Zodiac, is like a mammoth address system for any body in the sky. At any given moment, the planets can all be located at a specific point along this path.

How does this affect *you?* Well, a great part of your character—in fact, the central thread of your whole being—is described by that section of the Zodiac that the Sun occupied when you were born. Each sign of the Zodiac has certain basic traits associated with it. Since the Sun remains in each sign for about thirty days, that divides the population into twelve major character types. Of course, not everybody born the same month will have the same character, but you'll be amazed at how many fundamental traits you share with your astrological cousins of the same birth sign, no matter how many environmental differences you boast. The dates on which the Sun changes sign will vary from year

YOUR HOROSCOPE AND THE ZODIAC / 53

to year; that is why many people born near the cusp, or edge, of a sign often have difficulty determining which is their sign without the aid of a professional astrologer who can plot precisely the Sun's apparent motion for any given year. These dates are fluid and change according to the motion of the Earth from year to year.

Here are the twelve signs of the Zodiac as western astrology has recorded them. Listed also are the symbols associated with them and the *approximate* dates when the Sun enters and exits each sign for the year 1993.*

ARIES	Ram	March 20–April 19
TAURUS	Bull	April 19–May 20
GEMINI	Twins	May 20–June 21
CANCER	Crab	June 21–July 22
LEO	Lion	July 22–August 22
VIRGO	Virgin	August 22–September 22
LIBRA	Scales	September 22–October 23
SCORPIO	Scorpion	October 23–November 21
SAGITTARIUS	Archer	November 21–December 21
CAPRICORN	Sea-Goat	December 21–January 19
AQUARIUS	Water-Bearer	January 19–February 18
PISCES	Fish	February 18–March 20

*These dates are fluid and change with the motion of the Earth from year to year.

THE SIGNS OF THE ZODIAC

The signs of the Zodiac are an ingenious and complex summary of human behavioral and physical types, handed down from generation to generation through the bodies of all people in their hereditary material and through their minds. On the following pages you will find brief descriptions of all twelve signs in their highest and most ideal expression.

ARIES
The Sign of the Ram

Aries is the first sign of the Zodiac, and marks the beginning of springtime and the birth of the year. In spring the Earth begins its ascent upward and tips its North Pole toward the Sun. During this time the life-giving force of the Sun streams toward Earth, bathing our planet with the kiss of warmth and life. Plants start growing. Life wakes up. No more waiting. No more patience. The message has come from the Sun: Time to live!

Aries is the sign of the Self and is the crusade for the right of an individual to live in unimpeachable freedom. It represents the supremacy of the human will over all obstacles, limitations and threats. In Aries there is unlimited energy, optimism and daring, for it is the pioneer in search of a new world. It is the story of success and renewal, championship and victory. It is the living spirit of resilience and the power to be yourself, free from all restrictions and conditioning. There is no pattern you *have* to repeat, nobody's rule you just *have* to follow.

Confidence and positive action are born in Aries, and with little thought or fear of the past. Life is as magic as sunrise, with all the creative potential ahead of you for a new day. Activity, energy and adventure characterize this sign. In this sector of the Zodiac there is amazing strength, forthrightness, honesty and a stubborn refusal to accept defeat. The Aries nature is warm-blooded and forgiving, persuasive, masterful and decisive.

In short, Aries is the magic spark of life and being, the source of all initiative, courage, independence and self-esteem.

TAURUS
The Sign of the Bull

Taurus is wealth. It is not just money, property and the richness of material possessions, but also a wealth of the spirit. Taurus rules everything in the visible world we see, touch, hear, smell and taste—the Earth, sea and sky—everything we normally consider "real." It is the sign of economy and reserve, for it is a mixture of thrift and luxury, generosity and practicality. It is a blend of the spiritual and material, for the fertility of the sign is unlimited, and in this sense it is the mystical bank of life. Yet it must hold the fruit of its efforts in its hands and seeks to realize its fantasy-rich imagination with tangible rewards.

Loyalty and *endurance* make this sign perhaps the most stable of all. We can lean on Taurus, count on it, and it makes our earthly lives comfortable, safe and pleasurable. It is warm, sensitive, loving and capable of magnificent, joyful sensations. It is conservative and pragmatic, with a need to be sure of each step forward.

56 / THE SIGNS OF THE ZODIAC

It is the capacity to plan around eventualities without living in the future. Steadfast and constant, this is a sturdy combination of ruggedness and beauty, gentleness and unshakeability of purpose. It is the point at which we join body and soul. Unselfish friend and loyal companion, Taurus is profoundly noble and openly humanitarian. Tenacity and concentration slow the energy down to bring certain long-lasting rewards.

Taurus is a fertile resource and rich ground to grow in, and we all need it for our ideas and plans to flourish. It is the uncut diamond, symbolizing rich, raw tastes and a deep need for satisfaction, refinement and completion.

GEMINI
The Sign of the Twins

Gemini is the sign of mental brilliance. Communication is developed to a high degree of fluidity, rapidity, fluency. It is the chance for expressing ideas and relaying information from one place to another. Charming, debonair and lighthearted, it is a symbol of universal interest and eternal curiosity. The mind is quick and advanced, has a lightning-like ability to assimilate data.

It is the successful manipulation of verbal or visual language and the capacity to meet all events with objectivity and intelligence. It is light, quick wit, with a comic satiric twist. Gemini is the sign of writing or speaking.

It is the willingness to try anything once, with a need to wander and explore, the quick shifting of moods and attitudes being a basic characteristic that indicates a need for change. Versatility is the remarkable Gemini attribute. It is the capacity to investigate, perform and relate over great areas for short periods of time and thus to connect all areas. It is mastery of design and perception, the power to conceptualize and create by putting elements together—people, colors, patterns. It is the reporter's mind, plus a brilliant ability to see things in objective, colorful arrangement. Strength lies in constant refreshment of outlook and joyful participation in all aspects of life.

Gemini is involvement with neighbors, family and relatives, telephones, arteries of news and communication —anything that enhances the human capacity for communication and self-expression. It is active, positive and energetic, with an insatiable hunger for human interchange. Through Gemini bright and dark sides of personality merge and the mind has wings. As it flies it reflects the light of a boundless shining intellect. It is the development of varied talents from recognition of the duality of self.

Gemini is geared toward enjoying life to the fullest by finding, above all else, a means of expressing the inner self to the outside world.

CANCER
The Sign of the Crab

Cancer is the special relationship to *home* and involvement with the family unit. Maintaining harmony in the domestic sphere or improving conditions there is a major characteristic in this sector of the Zodiac. Cancer is attachment between two beings vibrating in sympathy with one another.

It is the comfort of a loving embrace, a tender generosity. Cancer is the place of shelter whenever there are lost or hungry souls in the night. Through Cancer we are fed, protected, comforted and soothed. When the coldness of the world threatens, Cancer is there with gentle understanding. It is protection and understated loyalty, a medium of rich, living feeling that is both psychic and mystical. Highly intuitive, Cancer has knowledge that other signs do not possess. It is the wisdom of the soul.

It prefers the quiet contentment of the home and hearth to the busy search for earthly success and civilized pleasures. Still, there is a respect for worldly knowledge. Celebration of life comes through food. The sign is the muted light of warmth, security and gladness, and its presence means *nourishment*. It rules fertility and the instinct to populate and raise young. It is growth of the soul. It is the ebb and flow of all our tides of feeling, involvements, habits and customs.

Through Cancer is reflected the inner condition of all human beings, and therein lies the seed of knowledge out of which the soul will grow.

LEO
The Sign of the Lion

Leo is love. It represents the warmth, strength and regeneration we feel through love. It is the radiance of lifegiving light and the center of all attention and activity. It is passion, romance, adventure and games. Pleasure, amusement, fun and entertainment are all part of Leo. Based on the capacity for creative feeling and the desire to express love, Leo is the number 1 sign. It represents the unlimited outpouring of all that is warm and positive.

It is loyalty, dignity, responsibility and command. Pride and nobility belong to Leo, and the dashing image of the knight in shining armor, pioneer or hero all are part of Leo. It is a sense of high honor and kingly generosity born out of deep, noble love. It is the excitement of the sportsman, with all the unbeatable flair and style of success. It is a strong, unyielding will and true sense of personal justice, a respect for human freedom and an enlightened awareness of people's needs.

Leo is involvement in the Self's awareness of personal talents and the desire and need to express them. At best it is forthrightness, courage and efficiency, authority and dignity, showmanship and a talent for organization. Dependable and ardent, the Lion is characterized by individuality, positivism and integrity.

It is the embodiment of human maturity, the effective individual in society, a virile creative force able to take chances and win. It is the love of laughter and the joy of making others happy. Decisive and enthusiastic, the Lion is the creative producer of the Zodiac. It is the potential to light the way for others.

VIRGO

The Sign of the Virgin

Virgo is the sign of work and service. It is the symbol of the farmer at harvest time, and represents tireless efforts for the benefit of humanity, the joy of bringing the fruits of the Earth to the table of mankind. Celebration through work is the characteristic of this sign. Sincerity, zeal, discipline and devotion mark the sign of the Virgin.

The key word is *purity,* and in Virgo lies a potential for unlimited self-mastery. Virgo is the embodiment of perfected skill and refined talent. The thread of work is woven into the entire life of Virgo. All creativity is poured into streamlining a job, classifying a system, eradicating unnecessary elements of pure analysis. The true Virgo genius is found in separating the wheat from the chaff.

Spartan simplicity characterizes this sign, and Virgo battles the war between order and disorder. The need to arrange, assimilate and categorize is great; it is the symbol of the diagnostician, the nurse and the healer. Criticism and analysis describe this sign—pure, incisive wisdom and a shy appreciation of life's joys. All is devoted to the attainment of perfection and the ideal of self-mastery.

Virgo is the sign of health and represents the physical body as a functioning symbol of the mental and spiritual planes. It is the state of healing the ills of the human being with natural, temperate living. It is maturation of the ego as it passes from a self-centered phase to its awareness and devotion to humanity.

It is humanitarian, pragmatic and scientific, with boundless curiosity. Focus and clarity of mind are the strong points, while strength of purpose and shy reserve underlie the whole sign. This is separateness, aloofness and solitude for this beacon of the Zodiac. As a lighthouse guides ships, so Virgo shines.

LIBRA
The Sign of the Scales

Libra is the sign of human relationship, marriage, equality and justice. It symbolizes the need of one human being for another, the capacity to find light, warmth and life-giving love in relationship to another human being. It is union on any level—mental, sexual, emotional or business. It is self-extension in a desire to find a partner with whom to share our joys. It is the capacity to recognize the needs of others and to develop to the fullest our powers of diplomacy, good taste and refinement.

Libra is harmony, grace, aesthetic sensibility, and the personification of the spirit of companionship. It represents the skill in maintaining balances and the ability to share mutually of all life's benefits, trials, crises and blessings. Libra is mastery at anticipation of another's needs or reactions. It is the exercise of simple justice with impartial delicacy.

It is the need to relate, to find a major person, place or thing to sustain us and draw out our attention. It is growth through becoming awakened to the outside world and other people. It is the union of two loving souls in honesty, equality, mutual cooperation and mutual accord.

SCORPIO
The Sign of the Scorpion

Scorpio is the sign of dark intensity, swirling passion and sexual magnetism. It is the thirst for survival and primitive animal drives which are the bases of sexual orientation and the creative impulses for self-expression. No other sign has such a profound instinct for survival and reproduction. Out of the abyss of emotions come a thousand creations, each one possessing a life of its own.

Scorpio is completion, determination and endurance, fortified with enough stamina to outlive any enemy. It is the pursuit of goals despite any threat, warning or obstacle that might stand in the way. It simply cannot be stopped. It knows when to wait and when to proceed. It is the constant state of readiness, a vibrant living force that constantly pumps out its rhythm from the depths of being.

Secretive and intimate, Scorpio symbolizes the self-directed creature with a will of steel. It is the flaming desire to create, manipulate and control with a magician's touch. But the most mysterious quality is the capacity for metamorphosis, or total transformation.

This represents supremacy in the battle with dark unseen forces. It is the state of being totally fearless—the embodiment of truth and courage. The healer. It symbolizes the human capacity to face all danger and emerge supreme. As a caterpillar spins its way into the darkness of a cocoon, Scorpio faces the end of existence, says goodbye to an old way of life and goes through a kind of death—or total change.

Then, amid the dread of uncertainty, something remarkable happens. From hopelessness or personal crisis a new individual emerges, like a magnificent butterfly leaving behind its cocoon. It is a human being completely transformed and victorious. This is Scorpio.

SAGITTARIUS
The Sign of the Archer

Sagittarius is the sign of adventure and a thousand and one new experiences. It is the cause and purpose of every new attempt at adventure or self-understanding. It is the embodiment of enthusiasm, search for truth and love of wisdom. Hope and optimism characterize this section of the Zodiac, and it is the ability to leave the past behind and set out again with positive resilience and a happy, cheerful outlook.

It is intelligence and exuberance, youthful idealism and the desire to expand all horizons. It is the constant hatching of dreams, the hunger for knowledge, travel and experience. The goal is exploration itself.

Sagittarius is generosity, humor and goodness of nature, backed up by the momentum of great expectations. It symbolizes the ability of people to be back in the race after having the most serious spills over the biggest hurdles. It is a healthy, positive outlook and the capacity to meet each new moment with unaffected buoyancy.

At this point in the Zodiac, greater conscious understanding begins to develop self-awareness and self-acceptance. It is an Olympian capacity to look upon the bright side and to evolve that aspect of mind we call conscience.

CAPRICORN
The Sign of the Sea-Goat

Capricorn is the sign of structure and physical law. It rules depth, focus and concentration. It is the symbol of success through perseverance, happiness through profundity. It is victory over disruption, and finds reality in codes set up by society and culture. It is the perpetuation of useful, tested patterns and a desire to protect what has already been established.

It is cautious, conservative, conscious of the passage of time, yet ageless. The Goat symbolizes the incorporation of reason into living and depth into loving. Stability, responsibility and fruitfulness through loyalty color this sector of the Zodiac with an undeniable and irrepressible awareness of success, reputation and honor. Capricorn is the culmination of our earthly dreams, the pinnacle of our worldly life.

It is introspection and enlightenment through serious contemplation of the Self and its position in the world. It is mastery of understanding and the realization of dreams.

Capricorn is a winter blossom, a born professional with an aim of harmony and justice, beauty, grace and success. It is the well-constructed pyramid: perfect and beautiful, architecturally correct, mysteriously implacable and hard to know. Highly organized and built on precise foundations to last and last and last. Practical, useful yet magnificent and dignified, signifying permanence and careful planning. Like a pyramid, Capricorn has thick impenetrable walls, complex passageways and false corridors. Yet somewhere at the heart of this ordered structure is the spirit of a mighty ruler.

AQUARIUS
The Sign of the Water-Bearer

Aquarius is the symbol of idealized free society. It is the herding instinct in man as a social animal. It is the collection of heterogeneous elements of human consciousness in coherent peaceful coexistence. Friendship, goodwill and harmonious contact are Aquarius attributes. It is founded on the principle of individual freedom and the brotherly love and respect for the rights of all men and women on Earth.

It is strength of will and purpose, altruism and love of human fellowship. It is the belief in spontaneity and free choice, in the openness to live in a spirit of harmony and cooperation—liberated from restriction, repression and conventional codes of conduct. It is the brilliant capacity to assimilate information instantaneously at the last minute and translate that information into immediate creative action, and thus to live in unpredictability.

This is the progressive mind, the collective mind—groups of people getting together to celebrate life. Aquarius is the child of the future, the utopian working for the betterment of the human race. Funds, charities, seeking better cities and better living conditions for others, involvement in great forms of media or communication, science or research in the hope of joining mankind to his higher self—this is all Aquarius.

It is invention, genius, revolution, discovery—instantaneous breakthrough from limitations. It's a departure from convention, eccentricity, the unexpected development that changes the course of history. It is the discovery of people and all the arteries that join them together. Aquarius is adventure, curiosity, exotic and alien appeal. It pours the water of life and intelligence for all humanity to drink. It is humanism, fraternity and the element of surprise.

PISCES
The Sign of the Fishes

Pisces is faith—undistracted, patient, all-forgiving faith—and therein lies the Pisces capacity for discipline, endurance and stamina.

It is imagination and other-worldliness, the condition of living a foggy, uncertain realm of poetry, music and fantasy. Passive and compassionate, this sector of the Zodiac symbolizes the belief in the inevitability of life. It represents the view of life that everything exists in waves, like the sea. All reality as we know it is a dream, a magic illusion that must ultimately be washed away. Tides pull this way and that, whirlpools and undercurrents sweep across the bottom of life's existence, but in Pisces there is total acceptance of all tides, all rhythms, all possibilities. It is the final resolution of all personal contradictions and all confusing paradoxes.

It is the search for truth and honesty, and the devotion to love, utterly and unquestionably. It is the desire to act with wisdom, kindness and responsibility and to welcome humanity completely free from scorn, malice, discrimination or prejudice. It is total, all-embracing, idealistic love. It is the acceptance of two sides of a question at once and love through sacrifice.

Pisces is beyond reality. We are here today, but may be gone tomorrow. Let the tide of circumstances carry you where it will, for nothing is forever. As all things come, so must they go. In the final reel, all things must pass away. It is deliverance from sorrow through surrender to the infinite. The emotions are as vast as the ocean, yet in the pain of confusion there is hope in the secret cell of one's own heart. Pisces symbolizes liberation from pain through love, faith and forgiveness.

THE SIGNS OF THE ZODIAC / 67

THE SIGNS AND THEIR KEY WORDS

		Positive	Negative
ARIES	self	courage, initiative, pioneer instinct	brash rudeness, selfish impetuosity
TAURUS	money	endurance, loyalty, wealth	obstinacy, gluttony
GEMINI	mind	versatility, communication	capriciousness, unreliability
CANCER	family	sympathy, homing instinct	clannishness, childishness
LEO	children	love, authority, integrity	egotism, force
VIRGO	work	purity, industry, analysis	fault-finding, cynicism
LIBRA	marriage	harmony, justice	vacillation, superficiality
SCORPIO	sex	survival, regeneration	vengeance, discord
SAGITTARIUS	travel	optimism, higher learning	lawlessness
CAPRICORN	career	depth, responsibility	narrowness, gloom
AQUARIUS	friends	humanity, genius	perverse unpredictability
PISCES	confinement	spiritual love, universality	diffusion, escapism

THE ELEMENTS AND THE QUALITIES OF THE SIGNS

ELEMENT	SIGN	QUALITY	SIGN
FIRE	ARIES LEO SAGITTARIUS	CARDINAL	ARIES LIBRA CANCER CAPRICORN
EARTH	TAURUS VIRGO CAPRICORN	FIXED	TAURUS LEO SCORPIO AQUARIUS
AIR	GEMINI LIBRA AQUARIUS	MUTABLE	GEMINI VIRGO SAGITTARIUS PISCES
WATER	CANCER SCORPIO PISCES		

Every sign has both an element and a quality associated with it. The element indicates the basic makeup of the sign, and the quality describes the kind of activity associated with each.

Signs can be grouped together according to their *element* and *quality*. Signs of the same element share many basic traits in common. They tend to form stable configurations and ultimately harmonious relationships. Signs of the same quality are often less harmonious, but share many dynamic potentials for growth and profound fulfillment.

THE SIGNS OF THE ZODIAC / 69
THE FIRE SIGNS

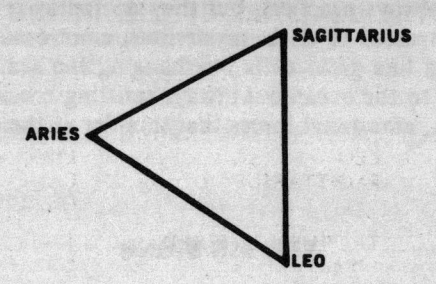

```
              SAGITTARIUS
ARIES
              LEO
```

This is the fire group. On the whole these are emotional, volatile types, quick to anger, quick to forgive. They are adventurous, powerful people and act as a source of inspiration for everyone. They spark into action with immediate exuberant impulses. They are intelligent, self-involved, creative and idealistic. They all share a certain vibrancy and glow that outwardly reflects an inner flame and passion for living.

THE EARTH SIGNS

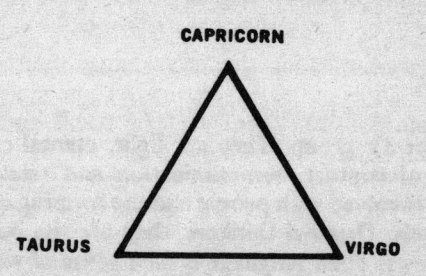

```
         CAPRICORN

TAURUS              VIRGO
```

This is the earth group. They are in constant touch with the material world and tend to be conservative. Although they are all capable of spartan self-discipline, they are earthy, sensual people who are stimulated by the tangible, elegant and luxurious. The thread of their lives is always practical, but they do fantasize and are often attracted to dark, mysterious, emotional people. They are like great cliffs overhanging the sea, forever married to the ocean but always resisting erosion from the dark, emotional forces that thunder at their feet.

THE AIR SIGNS

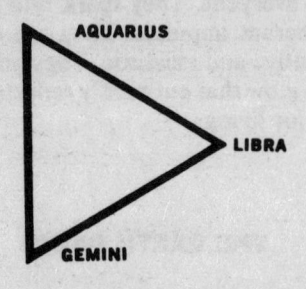

```
       AQUARIUS


                    LIBRA


       GEMINI
```

This is the air group. They are light, mental creatures desirous of contact, communication and relationship. They are involved with people and the forming of ties on many levels. Original thinkers, they are the bearers of human news. Their language is their sense of word, color, style and beauty. They provide an atmosphere suitable and pleasant for living. They add change and versatility to the scene, and it is through them that we can explore human intelligence and experience.

THE WATER SIGNS

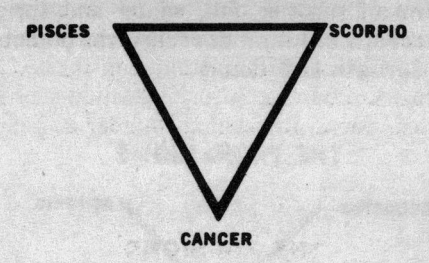

```
     PISCES          SCORPIO
         \          /
          \        /
           \      /
            \    /
             \  /
            CANCER
```

This is the water group. Through the water people, we are all joined together on emotional, non-verbal levels. They are silent, mysterious types whose magic hypnotizes even the most determined realist. They have uncanny perceptions about people and are as rich as the oceans when it comes to feeling, emotion or imagination. They are sensitive, mystical creatures with memories that go back beyond time. Through water, life is sustained. These people have the potential for the depths of darkness or the heights of mysticism and art.

THE CARDINAL SIGNS

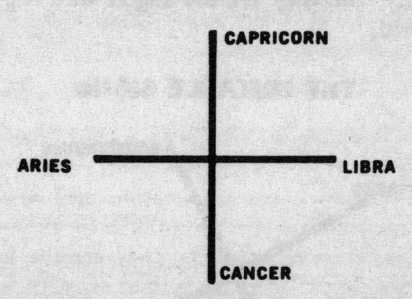

```
            CAPRICORN
               |
               |
ARIES ─────────┼───────── LIBRA
               |
               |
             CANCER
```

Put together, this is a clear-cut picture of dynamism, activity, tremendous stress and remarkable achievement. These people know the meaning of great change since their lives are often characterized by significant crises and major successes. This combination is like a simultaneous storm of summer, fall, winter and spring. The danger is chaotic diffusion of energy; the potential is irrepressible growth and victory.

THE FIXED SIGNS

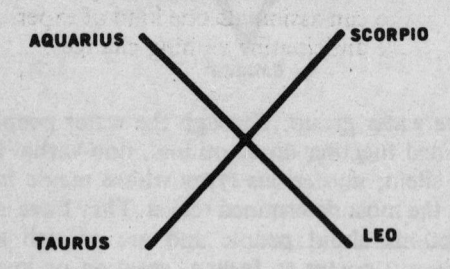

```
AQUARIUS          SCORPIO
        \        /
         \      /
          \    /
           \  /
            \/
            /\
           /  \
          /    \
         /      \
        /        \
TAURUS            LEO
```

Fixed signs are always establishing themselves in a given place or area of experience. Like explorers who arrive and plant a flag, these people claim a position from which they do not enjoy being deposed. They are staunch, stalwart, upright, trusty, honorable people, although their obstinacy is well-known. Their contribution is fixity, and they are the angels who support our visible world.

THE MUTABLE SIGNS

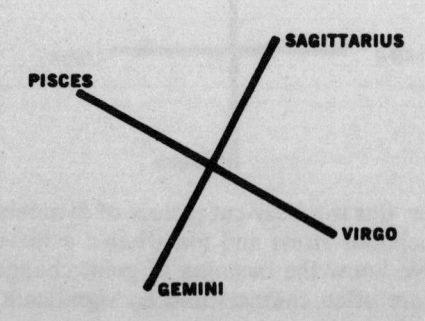

```
                SAGITTARIUS
               /
    PISCES    /
        \    /
         \  /
          \/
          /\
         /  \
        /    \
       /      VIRGO
      /
   GEMINI
```

Mutable people are versatile, sensitive, intelligent, nervous and deeply curious about life. They are the translators of all energy. They often carry out or complete tasks initiated by others. Combinations of these signs have highly developed minds; they are imaginative and jumpy and think and talk a lot. At worst their lives are a Tower of Babel. At best they are adaptable and ready creatures who can assimilate one kind of experience and enjoy it while anticipating coming changes.

THE ZODIAC AND THE HUMAN BODY

The signs of the Zodiac are linked to the human body in a direct relationship. Each sign has a part of the body with which it is associated.

It is traditionally believed that surgery is best performed when the Moon is passing through a sign *other* than the sign associated with the part of the body upon which an operation is to be performed. But often the presence of the Moon in a particular sign will bring the focus of attention to that very part of the body under medical scrutiny.

The principles of medical astrology are complex and beyond the scope of this introduction. We can, however, list the signs of the Zodiac and the parts of the human body connected with them. Once you learn these correspondences, you'll be amazed at how accurate they are.

ARIES	Head, brain, face, upper jaw
TAURUS	Throat, neck, lower jaw
GEMINI	Hands, arms, lungs, nerves
CANCER	Stomach, breasts, womb, liver
LEO	Heart, spine
VIRGO	Intestines, liver
LIBRA	Kidneys, lower back
SCORPIO	Sex and eliminative organs
SAGITTARIUS	Hips, thighs, liver
CAPRICORN	Skin, bones, teeth, knees
AQUARIUS	Circulatory system, lower legs
PISCES	Feet, tone of being

HOW TO APPROXIMATE YOUR RISING SIGN

Apart from the month and day of birth, the exact time of birth is another vital factor in the determination of an accurate horoscope. Not only do planets move with great speed, but one must know how far the Earth has turned during the day. That way you can determine exactly where the planets are located with respect to the precise birthplace of an individual. This makes your horoscope *your* horoscope. In addition to these factors, another grid is laid upon that of the Zodiac and the planets: the houses. After all three have been considered, specific planetary relationships can be measured and analyzed in accordance with certain ordered procedures. It is the skillful translation of all this complex astrological language that serious astrologers strive for in their attempt at coherent astrological synthesis. Keep this in mind.

The horoscope sets up a kind of framework around which the life of an individual grows like wild ivy, this way and that, weaving its way around the trellis of the natal positions of the planets. The year of birth tells us the positions of the distant, slow-moving planets like Jupiter, Saturn, Uranus and Pluto. The month of birth indicates the Sun sign, or birth sign as it is commonly called, as well as indicating the positions of the rapidly moving planets like Venus, Mercury and Mars. The day of birth locates the position of our Moon, and the moment of birth determines the houses through what is called the Ascendant, or Rising sign.

As the Earth rotates on its axis once every 24 hours,

each one of the twelve signs of the Zodiac appears to be "rising" on the horizon, with a new one appearing about every two hours. Actually it is the turning of the Earth that exposes each sign to view, but you will remember that in much of our astrological work we are discussing "apparent" motion. This Rising sign marks the Ascendant and it colors the whole orientation of a horoscope. It indicates the sign governing the first house of the chart, and will thus determine which signs will govern all the other houses. The idea is a bit complicated at first, and we needn't dwell on complications in this introduction. But if you can imagine two color wheels with twelve divisions superimposed upon each other, one moving slowly and the other remaining still, you will have some idea of how the signs keep shifting the "color" of the houses as the Rising sign continues to change every two hours.

The important point is that the birth chart, or horoscope, actually does define specific factors of a person's makeup. It contains a picture of being, much the way the nucleus of a tiny cell contains the potential for an entire elephant, or a packet of seeds contains a rosebush. If there were no order or continuity to the world, we could plant roses and get elephants. This same order that gives continuous flow to our lives often annoys people if it threatens to determine too much of their lives. We must grow from what we were planted, and there's no reason why we can't do that magnificently. It's all there in the horoscope. Where there is limitation, there is breakthrough; where there is crisis, there is transformation. Accurate analysis of a horoscope can help you find these points of breakthrough and transformation, and it requires knowledge of subtleties and distinctions that demand skillful judgment in order to solve even the simplest kind of personal question.

It is still quite possible, however, to draw some conclusions based upon the sign occupied by the Sun alone.

HOW TO APPROXIMATE YOUR RISING SIGN / 77

In fact, if you're just being introduced to this vast subject, you're better off keeping it simple. Otherwise it seems like an impossible jumble, much like trying to read a novel in a foreign language without knowing the basic vocabulary. As with anything else, you can progress in your appreciation and understanding of astrology in direct proportion to your interest. To become really good at it requires study, experience, patience and above all—and maybe simplest of all—a fundamental understanding of what is actually going on right up there in the sky over your head. It is a vital living process you can observe, contemplate and ultimately understand. You can start by observing sunrise, or sunset, or even the Full Moon.

In fact you can do a simple experiment after reading this introduction. You can erect a rough chart by following the simple procedure below. Refer to the diagram on the next page to see what a completed chart for an individual—someone who was born at 5:15 pm on October 31 in New York City—actually looks like. Then follow the steps below to make your own chart.

1. Draw a circle with twelve equal segments.
2. Starting at what would be the nine o'clock position on a clock, number the segments, or houses, from 1 to 12 in a *counterclockwise direction*.
3. Label house number 1 in the following way: 4 A.M.—6 A.M.
4. In a counterclockwise direction, label the rest of the houses: 2 A.M.—4 A.M., Midnight—2 A.M., 10 P.M.—Midnight, 8 P.M.—10 P.M., 6 P.M.—8 P.M., 4 P.M.— 6 P.M., 2 P.M.—4 P.M., Noon—2 P.M., 10 A.M.—Noon, 8 A.M.—10 A.M., and 6 A.M.—8 A.M.
5. Now find out what time you were born and place the sun in the appropriate house.
6. Label the edge of that house with your Sun sign.
7. Now label the rest of the houses with the signs,

78 / HOW TO APPROXIMATE YOUR RISING SIGN

starting with your Sun sign, in order, still in a *counterclockwise direction*. When you get to Pisces, start over with Aries and keep going until you reach the house behind the Sun.

8. Look to house number 1. The sign that you have now labeled and attached to house number 1 is your Rising sign. It will color your self-image, outlook, physical constitution, early life and whole orientation to life.

When you get through labeling all the houses, your drawing should look something like the diagram below. This diagram was constructed for an individual born at 5:15 P.M. on October 31 in New York City. The Sun is in Scorpio and is found in the 7th house. The Rising sign, or the sign governing house number 1, is Taurus, so this person is a blend of Scorpio and Taurus.

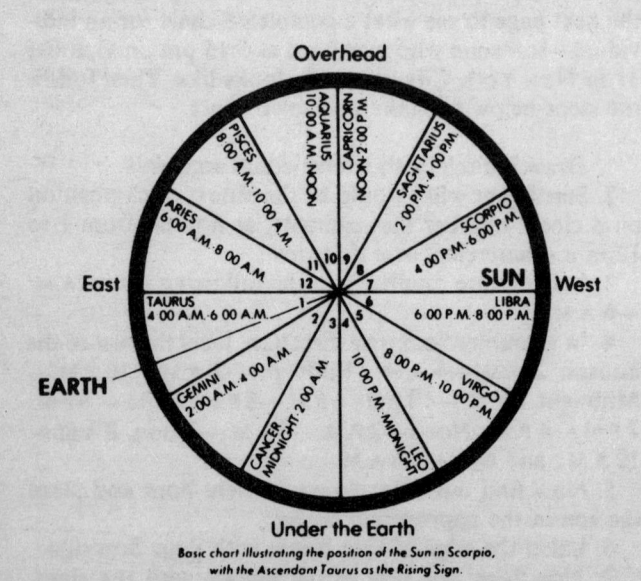

Basic chart illustrating the position of the Sun in Scorpio, with the Ascendant Taurus as the Rising Sign.

HOW TO APPROXIMATE YOUR RISING SIGN / 79

Your completed diagram of your own birth chart is, of course, just a mere approximation, since there are many complicated calculations that must be made with respect to adjustments for birth time. If you read descriptions of the sign preceding and the sign following the one you have calculated in the above manner, you may be able to identify yourself better.

Any further calculation would necessitate that you look in an ephemeris, or table of planetary motion, for the positions of the rest of the planets for your particular birth year.

We will leave such mathematics and go on to the next section. There we will list the meanings of the various houses, so you can better understand the position of your Sun. The house where your Sun sign is gives you a description of your basic character and your fundamental drives. You can also see in what areas of life on Earth you will be most likely to focus your constant energy and center your activity.

In the section after the houses, we will also take the time to define briefly all the known planets of our Solar System, the Sun, and the Moon, to acquaint you with more of the astrological vocabulary that you will be meeting again and again.

THE HOUSES AND THEIR MEANINGS

The twelve houses of every horoscope represent areas of life on Earth, or regions of worldly experience. Depending on which sign of the Zodiac was rising on the eastern horizon at the moment of birth, the activity of each house will be "colored" by the zodiacal sign on its cusp, or edge. In other words, the sign falling on the first house will determine what signs will fall on the rest of the houses.

1   The first house determines the basic orientation to all of life on Earth. It indicates the body type, face, head and brain. It rules your self-image, or the way others see you because of the way you see your self. This is the Ascendant of the horoscope and is the focus of energies of your whole chart. It acts like a prism through which all of the planetary light passes and is reflected in your life. It colors your outlook and influences everything you do and see.

2   This is the house of finances. Here is your approach to money and materialism in general. It indicates where the best sources are for you to improve your financial condition and your earning power as a whole. It describes your values, alliances and assets.

3   This is the house of the day-to-day mind. Short trips, communication and transportation are associated with this house. It deals with routines, brothers and sisters, relatives, neighbors and the near environment at hand. Language, letters and the tools for transmitting information are included in third-house matters.

4   This is the house that describes your home and

homelife, parents, and childhood in the sense of indicating the kind of roots you come from. It symbolizes your present home and domestic situation and reflects your need for privacy and retreat from the world, indicating, of course, what kind of scene you require.

5 Pleasure, love affairs, amusements, parties, creativity, children. This is the house of passion and courtship and of expressing your talents, whatever they are. It is related to the development of your personal life and the capacity to express feeling and enjoy romance.

6 This is the house of work. Here there are tasks to be accomplished and maladjustments to be corrected. It is the house of health as well, and describes some of the likely places where physical health difficulties may appear. It rules routines, regimen, necessary jobs as opposed to a chosen career, army, navy, police—people employed, co-workers and those in service to others. It indicates the individual's ability to harvest the fruit of his own efforts.

7 This is the house of marriage, partnership and unions. It represents the alter ego, all people other than yourself, open confrontation with the public. It describes your partner and the condition of partnership as you discern it. In short, it is your "take" on the world. It indicates your capacity to make the transition from courtship to marriage and specifically what you seek out in others.

8 This is the house of deep personal transition, sex as a form of mutual surrender and interchange between human beings. It is the release from tensions and the completion of the creative processes. The eighth house also has to do with taxes, inheritances and the finances of others, as well as death as the ending of cycles and crises.

82 / THE HOUSES AND THEIR MEANINGS

9 This is the house of the higher mind, philosophy, religion and the expression of personal conscience through moral codes. It indicates religious leanings, ethical views and the capacity of the individual for a broader perspective and deeper understanding of himself. It is through the ninth house that you make great strides in learning and travel to distant places and come to know yourself through study, dreams and wide experience.

10 This is the house of career, honor and prestige. It marks the culmination of worldly experience and indicates the highest point you can reach, what you look up to, and how high you can go in this lifetime. It describes your parents, employers and how you view authority figures in general, the condition and direction of your profession and your position in the community.

11 This is the house of friendships. It describes your social behavior, your views on humanity and your hopes, aspirations and wishes for an ideal life. It will indicate what kinds of groups, clubs, organizations and friendships you tend to form and what you seek out in your chosen alliances other than with your mate or siblings. This house suggests the capacity for the freedom and unconventionality that an individual is seeking, his sense of his connection with mankind and the definition of his goals, personal and social.

12 This is the house of seclusion, secret wisdom and self-incarceration. It indicates our secret enemies as well, in the sense that there may be persons, feelings or memories we are trying to escape. It is self-undoing in that this house acts against the ego in order to find a higher, more universal purpose. It rules prisons, hospitals, charities and selfless service. It is the house of unfinished psychic business.

THE PLANETS OF THE SOLAR SYSTEM

Here are the planets of the Solar System. They all travel around the Sun at different speeds and different distances. Taken with the Sun, they all distribute individual intelligence and ability throughout the entire chart.

The planets modify the influence of the Sun in a chart according to their own particular natures, strengths and positions. Their positions must be calculated for each year and day, and their function and expression in a horoscope will change as they move from one area of the Zodiac to another.

Following, you will find brief statements of their pure meanings.

THE SUN

The Sun is the center of existence. Around this flaming sphere all the planets revolve in endless orbits. Our star is constantly sending out its beams of light and energy without which no life on Earth would be possible. In astrology it symbolizes everything we are trying to become, the center around which all of our activity in life will always revolve. It is the symbol of our basic nature and describes the natural and constant thread that runs through everything that we do from birth to death on this planet.

THE SUN

Everything in the horoscope ultimately revolves

around this singular body. Although other forces may be prominent in the charts of some individuals, still the Sun is the total nucleus of being and symbolizes the complete potential of every human being alive. It is vitality and the life force. Your whole essence comes from the position of the Sun.

You are always trying to express the Sun according to its position by house and sign. Possibility for all development is found in the Sun, and it marks the fundamental character of your personal radiations all around you.

It symbolizes strength, vigor, ardor, generosity and the ability to function effectively as a mature individual and a creative force in society. It is consciousness of the gift of life. The undeveloped solar nature is arrogant, pushy, undependable and proud, and is constantly using force.

MERCURY

Mercury is the planet closest to the Sun. It races around our star, gathering information and translating it to the rest of the system. Mercury represents your capacity to understand the desires of your own will and to translate those desires into action.

MERCURY

In other words it is the planet of Mind and the power of communication. Through Mercury we develop an ability to think, write, speak and observe—to become aware of the world around us. It colors our attitudes and vision of the world, as well as our capacity to communicate our inner responses to the outside world. Some people who have serious disabilities in their power of verbal communication have often wrongly been described as people lacking intelligence.

Although this planet (and its position in the horoscope) indicates your power to communicate your thoughts and perceptions to the world, intelligence is something deeper. Intelligence is distributed throughout all the planets. It is the relationship of the planets to each other that truly describes what we call intelligence. Mercury rules speaking, language, mathematics, draft and design, students, messengers, young people, offices, teachers and any pursuits where the mind of man has wings.

VENUS

Venus is beauty. It symbolizes the harmony and radiance of a rare and elusive quality: beauty itself. It is refinement and delicacy, softness and charm. In astrology it indicates grace, balance and the esthetic sense. Where Venus is we see beauty, a gentle drawing in of energy and the need for satisfaction and completion. It is a special touch that finishes off rough edges.

VENUS

Venus is the planet of sensitivity, and affection, and it is always the place for that other elusive phenomenon: love. Venus describes our sense of what is beautiful and loving. Poorly developed, it is vulgar, tasteless and self-indulgent. But its ideal is the flame of spiritual love—Aphrodite, goddess of love, and the sweetness and power of personal beauty.

MARS

Mars is raw, crude energy. The planet next to Earth but outward from the Sun is a fiery red sphere that charges through the horoscope with force and fury. It represents the way you reach out for new adventure and new experience. It is energy and drive, initiative, courage and daring. The power to start something and see it through. It can be thoughtless, cruel and wild, angry and hostile, causing cuts, burns, scalds and wounds. It can stab its way through a chart, or it can be the symbol of healthy spirited adventure, well-channeled constructive power to begin and keep up the drive.

MARS

If you have trouble starting things, if you lack the get-up-and-go to start the ball rolling, if you lack aggressiveness and self-confidence, chances are there's another planet influencing your Mars. Mars rules soldiers, butchers, surgeons, salespeople—in general any field that requires daring, bold skill, operational technique or self-promotion.

JUPITER

Jupiter is the largest planet of the Solar System. Scientists have recently learned that Jupiter reflects more light than it receives from the Sun. In a sense it is like a star itself. In astrology it rules good luck and good cheer, health, wealth, optimism, happiness, success and joy. It is the symbol of opportunity and always opens the way for new possibilities in your life. It rules exuberance, enthusiasm, wisdom, knowledge, generosity and all forms of expansion in general. It rules actors, statesmen, clerics, professional people, religion, publishing and the distribution of many people over large areas.

JUPITER

Sometimes Jupiter makes you think you deserve everything, and you become sloppy, wasteful, careless and rude, prodigal and lawless, in the illusion that nothing can ever go wrong. Then there is the danger of your showing overconfidence, exaggeration, undependability and overindulgence.

Jupiter is the minimization of limitation and the emphasis on spirituality and potential. It is the thirst for knowledge and higher learing.

SATURN

Saturn circles our system in dark splendor with its mysterious rings, forcing us to be awakened to whatever we have neglected in the past. It will present real puzzles and problems to be solved, causing delays, obstacles and hindrances. By doing so, Saturn stirs our own sensitivity to those areas where we are laziest.

SATURN

Here we must patiently develop *method,* and only through painstaking effort can our ends be achieved. It brings order to a horoscope and imposes reason just where we are feeling least reasonable. By creating limitations and boundary, Saturn shows the consequences of being human and demands that we accept the changing

88 / THE PLANETS OF THE SOLAR SYSTEM

cycles inevitable in human life. Saturn rules time, old age and sobriety. It can bring depression, gloom, jealousy and greed, or serious acceptance of responsibilities out of which success will develop. With Saturn there is nothing to do but face facts. It rules laborers, stones, granite, rocks and crystals of all kinds.

THE OUTER PLANETS: URANUS, NEPTUNE, PLUTO

Uranus, Neptune, and Pluto are the outer planets. They liberate human beings from cultural conditioning, and in that sense are the law breakers. In early times it was thought that Saturn was the last planet of the system—the outer limit beyond which we could never go. The discovery of the next three planets ushered in new phases of human history, revolution and technology.

URANUS

Uranus rules unexpected change, upheaval, revolution. It is the symbol of total independence and asserts the freedom of an individual from all restriction and restraint. It is a breakthrough planet and indicates talent, originality and genius in a horoscope. It usually causes last-minute reversals and changes of plan, unwanted separations, accidents, catastrophes and eccentric behavior. It can add irrational rebelliousness and perverse bohemianism to a personality or a streak of unaffected brilliance in science and art.

URANUS

Uranus rules technology, aviation and all forms of electrical and electronic advancement. It governs great leaps forward and topsy-turvy situations, and *always* turns things around at the last minute. Its effects are difficult to ever really predict, since it rules sudden last-minute decisions and events that come like lightning out of the blue.

NEPTUNE

Neptune dissolves existing reality the way the sea erodes the cliffs beside it. Its effects are subtle like the ringing of a buoy's bell in the fog. It suggests a reality higher than definition can usually describe. It awakens a sense of higher responsibility often causing guilt, worry, anxieties or delusions. Neptune is associated with all forms of escape and can make things seem a certain way so convincingly that you are absolutely sure of something that eventually turns out to be quite different.

NEPTUNE

It is the planet of illusion and therefore governs the invisible realms that lie beyond our ordinary minds, beyond our simple factual ability to prove what is "real." Treachery, deceit, disillusionment and disappointment are linked to Neptune. It describes a vague reality that promises eternity and the divine, yet in a manner so complex that we cannot really fathom it at all. At its worst Neptune is a cheap intoxicant; at its best it is the poetry, music and inspiration of the higher planes of spiritual love. It has dominion over movies, photographs and much of the arts.

PLUTO

Pluto lies at the outpost of our system and therefore rules finality in a horoscope—the final closing of chapters in your life, the passing of major milestones and points of development from which there is no return. It is a final wipeout, a closeout, an evacuation. It is a distant, subtle but powerful catalyst in all transformations that occur. It creates, destroys, then recreates. Sometimes Pluto starts its influence with a minor event or insignificant incident that might even go unnoticed. Slowly but surely, little by little, everything changes, until at last there has been a total transformation in the area of your life where Pluto has been operating. It rules mass thinking and the trends that society first rejects, then adopts and finally outgrows.

PLUTO

Pluto rules the dead and the underworld—all the powerful forces of creation and destruction that go on all the time beneath, around and above us. It can bring a lust for power with strong obsessions.

It is the planet that rules the metamorphosis of the caterpillar into a butterfly, for it symbolizes the capacity to change totally and forever a person's life style, way of thought and behavior.

THE MOON

Exactly how does the Moon affect us psychologically and psychically? We know it controls the tides; we've already seen that. We understand how it affects blood rhythm and body tides, together with all the chemical fluids that constitute our physical selves. Astronauts have walked upon its surface, and our scientists are now

THE PLANETS OF THE SOLAR SYSTEM

studying and analyzing data that will help determine the age of our satellite, its origin and makeup.

THE MOON

But the true mystery of that small body as it circles our Earth each month remains hidden. Is it really a dead, lifeless body that has no light or heat of its own, reflecting only what the gigantic Sun throws toward it? Is it a sensitive reflecting device, which translates the blinding, billowing energy from our star into a language our bodies can understand?

In Astrology, the Moon is said to rule our feelings, customs, habits and moods. As the Sun is the constant, ever shining source of life in daytime, the Moon is our nighttime *mother,* lighting up the night and swiftly moving, reflecting ever so rapidly the changing phases of behavior and personality. If we feel happy or joyous, or we notice certain habits and repetitive feelings that bubble up from our dark centers then vanish as quickly as they appeared, very often it is the position of the Moon that describes these changes.

THE MOON IN ALL SIGNS

The Moon moves quickly through the Zodiac, that is, through all twelve signs of our Sun's apparent path. It takes approximately one month for the entire trip, staying in each sign for about 2½ days. During its brief stay in a given sign, the moods and responses of people are always colored by the nature of that sign, any planets located there at that time, or any other heavenly bodies placed in such a way that the Moon will pick up their "vibration" as well. It's astonishing to observe how clearly the Moon changes people's interests and involvements as it moves along.

The following section gives brief descriptions of the Moon's influence in each sign.

MOON IN ARIES

There's excitement in the air. Some new little thing appears, and people are quick and full of energy and enterprise, ready for something new and turning on to a new experience. There's not much patience for hesitation, doubt or preoccupation with guilty self-damning recriminations. What's needed is action. People feel like putting their plans into operation. Pleasure and adventure characterize the mood, and it's time for things to change, pick up, improve. Confidence, optimism and positive feeling pervade the air. Sick people take a turn for the better. Life stirs with a feeling of renewal. People react bravely to challenges, with a sense of courage and dynamism. Self-reliance is the key word, and people

THE MOON IN ALL SIGNS / 93

minimize their problems and maximize the power to exercise freedom of the will. There is an air of abruptness and shortness of consideration, but, at the same time, people are feeling the courage of their convictions to do something for themselves. Feelings are strong and intuitive, and the mood is idealistic and freedom-oriented.

MOON IN TAURUS

Here the mood is just as pleasure loving, but less idealistic. Now the concerns are more materialistic, money-oriented and down-to-earth. The mood is more stable, diligent, thoughtful and deliberate. It is a time when feelings are rich and deep, with a profound appreciation of the good things the world has to offer and the pleasures of the sensations. It is a period when people's minds are more serious, "realistic," and devoted to the increases and improvements of property and possessions and acquisition of wealth. It's a much more conservative tone, and people are more fixed in their views, sedentary and needing to add to their stability in every way. Assessment of assets, criticism and the execution of tasks are strong involvements of the Taurus Moon when financial matters demand attention. It is devotion to security on a financial and emotional level. It is a fertile time, when ideas can begin to take root and grow.

MOON IN GEMINI

There is a rapid increase in movement. People are moving around, exchanging ideas and information. Gossip and news travel fast under this Moon, because people are naturally involved with communication, finding out things from some, passing on information to others. Feelings shift to a more mental level now, and people feel and say things that are sincere at the moment but lack the root and depth to endure much beyond the moment. People are involved with short-term engagements, quick trips from here to there, and there is a definite need for changing the scene. You'll find people flirtatious and talkative, experimental and easygoing, falling into encounters they hadn't planned on. The mind is quick and active, with powers of writing and speaking greatly enhanced. Radio, television, letters, newspapers and magazines are in the spotlight with the Moon in Gemini, and new chances pop up for self-expression, with new people involved. Relatives and neighbors are tuned in to you and you to them. Take advantage of this fluidity of mind. It can rescue you from worldly involvements and get you into new surroundings for a short while.

MOON IN CANCER

Now you'll see people heading home. People are more likely to turn their attention inward to their place of residence under this position of the Moon. The active, changeable moods of yesterday vanish, and people settle in as if they were searching for a nest of security.

Actually people are retiring now, seeking to find peace and quiet within themselves. That's what they're feeling when they prefer to stay home rather than go out with a whole crowd of people to strange places. They need the warmth and comfort of the family and hearth. Maybe they feel anxious and insecure from the hustle and bustle of the workaday world. Maybe they're just "tired." But it's definitely a time of more tender need for emotional sustenance. It's a time for nostalgia and returning to times and places that once nourished you deeply. Thoughts of parents, family and old associations come to people. The heritage of their family ties holds them strongly now. These are personal needs that must be fed. Moods are deep and mysterious and sometimes sad. People are silent, psychic and imaginative during this period. It's a fruitful time when people respond to love, food and all the comforts of the inner world.

MOON IN LEO

The shift is back out in the world, and people are born again, like kids. They feel zestful, passionate, exuberant and need plenty of attention. They're interested in having a good time, enjoying themselves, and the world of entertainment takes over for a while. Places of amusement, theaters, parties, sprees, a whole gala of glamorous events, characterize this stage of the Moon's travel. Gracious, lavish hosting and a general feeling of buoyancy and flamboyance are in the air. It's a time of sunny, youthful fun when people are in the mood to take chances and win. The approach is direct, ardent and strong. Bossy, authoritarian feelings predominate, and people throw themselves forward for all they're worth. Flattery is rampant, but the ego is vibrant and flourishing with the kiss of life, romance and love. Speculation is indicated, and it's usually a time to go out and try your hand at love. Life is full and rich as a summer meadow, and feelings are warm.

MOON IN VIRGO

The party's over. Eyelashes are on the table. This is a time for cleaning up after the merrymakers have gone home. People are now concerned with sobering up and getting personal affairs straight, clearing up any confusions or undefined feelings from the night before, and generally attending to the practical business of doctoring up after the party. People are back at work, concerned with necessary, perhaps tedious tasks—paying bills, fixing and adjusting things and generally purifying their lives, streamlining their affairs and involving themselves with work and service to the community. Purity is the key word in personal habits, diet and emotional needs. Propriety and coolness take the place of yesterday's devil-may-care passion, and the results are a detached, inhibited period for the Moon. Feelings are not omitted; they are merely subjected to the scrutiny of the mind and thus purified. Health comes to the fore, and people are interested in clearing up problems.

MOON IN LIBRA

Here there is a mood of harmony, when people strive to join with other people in a bond of peace and justice. At this time people need relationships and often seek the company of others in a smooth-flowing feeling of love, beauty and togetherness. People make efforts to understand other people, and though it's not the best time to make decisions, many situations keep presenting themselves from the outside to change plans and offer new opportunities. There is a general search for accord between partners, and differences are explored as similarities are shared. The tone is conciliatory, and the mood is one of cooperation, patience and tolerance. People do not generally feel independent, and sometimes this need to share or lean on others disturbs them. It shouldn't. This is the moment for uniting and sharing, for feeling a mutual flow of kindness and tenderness between people. The air is ingratiating and sometimes lacks stamina, courage and a consistent, definite point of view. But it is a time favoring the condition of beauty and the development of esthetics.

MOON IN SCORPIO

This is not a mood of sharing. It's driving, intense, brooding and full of passion and desire. Its baser aspects are the impulses of selfishness, cruelty, and the pursuit of animal drives and appetites. There is a craving for excitement and a desire to battle and win in a bloodthirsty war for survival. It is competitive and ruthless, sarcastic and easily bruised, highly sexual and touchy, without being especially tender. Retaliation, jealousy and revenge can be felt too during this time. Financial involvements, debts and property issues arise now. Powerful underworld forces are at work here, and great care is needed to transform ignorance into wisdom, to keep the mind from descending into the lower depths. During the Moon's stay in Scorpio we contact the dark undercurrents swirling around and get in touch with a magical part of our natures. Interest lies in death, inheritance and the powers of rebirth and regeneration.

MOON IN SAGITTARIUS

Here the mind climbs out of the depths, and people are involved with the higher, more enlightened and conscious facets of their personality. There's a renewed interest in learning, education and philosophy, with a new involvement with ethics, morals, national and international issues: a concern with looking for a better way to live. It's a time of general improvement, with people feeling more deeply hopeful and optimistic. They are dreaming of new places, new possibilities, new horizons. They are emerging from the abyss and leaving the past behind, with their eyes out toward the new horizon. They decide to travel, or renew their contacts with those far away. They question their religious beliefs and investigate new areas of metaphysical inquiry. It's a time for adventure, sports, playing the field—people have their eye on new possibilities. They are bored with depression and details. They feel restless and optimistic, joyous and delighted to be alive. Thoughts revolve around adventure, travel, liberation.

MOON IN CAPRICORN

When the Moon moves into Capricorn things slow

down considerably. People require a quieter, more organized and regularized condition. Their minds are sober, more "realistic," and they are methodically going about bringing their dreams and plans into reality. They are more conscious of what is standing between them and success, and during this time they take definite, decisive steps to remove any obstacles from their path. They are cautious, suspicious, sometimes depressed, discouraged and gloomy, but they are more determined than ever to accomplish their tasks. They take care of responsibilities now, wake up to facts, and wrestle with problems and dilemmas of this world. They are politically minded and concerned with social convention now, and it is during this period that conditioning and conformity elicit the greatest responses. People are moderate and serious and surround themselves with what is most familiar. They want predictable situations and need time to think deeply and deliberately about all issues. It's a time for planning.

MOON IN AQUARIUS

Spontaneity replaces the sober predictability of yesterday. Now events, people and situations pop up, and you take advantage of unsought opportunities and can expect the unexpected. Surprises, reversals, and shifts in plans mark this period. There is a resurgence of optimism, and things you wouldn't expect to happen suddenly do. What you were absolutely sure was going to happen, simply doesn't. Here there is a need for adventure born from a healthy curiosity that characterizes people's moods. Unrealistic utopias are dreamed of, maybe, and it is from such idealistic dreams that worlds of the future are built. There is a renewed interest in friendship, comradeship, brotherly love and union on high planes of mental and spiritual companionship. People free each other from grudges or long-standing deadlocks, and there is a hopeful joining of hands in a spirit of love and peace. People don't feel like sticking to previous plans and they need to be able to respond to new situations at the last minute. People need freedom. Groups of people come together and meet, perhaps for a common purpose like having dinner or hearing music, and leave knowing each other better.

MOON IN PISCES

Flashes of brilliant insight and mysterious knowledge characterize this stage of the Moon's passage through the Zodiac. Sometimes valuable "truths" seem to emerge which, later in the light of day, turn out to be false. This is a time of poetry, intuition and music, when worldly realities can be the most illusory and unreliable of all. There are often feelings of remorse, guilt or sorrow connected with this Moon—sorrow from the childhood or family or past. Confusion, anxiety, worry and a host of imagined pains and sorrows may drag you down until you cannot move or think. Often there are connections with hospitals, prisons, alcohol, drugs and lower forms of escape. It is a highly emotional time, when the feelings and compassion for humanity and all people everywhere rise to the surface of your being. Mysteries of society and the soul now rise to demand solutions, but often the riddles posed during this period have many answers that all seem right. It is more a time for inner reflection than positive action. It is a time when poetry and music float to the surface of the being, and for the creative artist it is the richest source of his inspiration.

MOON TABLES

CORRECTION FOR NEW YORK TIME, FIVE HOURS WEST OF GREENWICH

Atlanta, Boston, Detroit, Miami, Washington, Montreal, Ottawa, Quebec, Bogota, Havana, Lima, Santiago	Same time
Chicago, New Orleans, Houston, Winnipeg, Churchill, Mexico City	Deduct 1 hour
Albuquerque, Denver, Phoenix, El Paso, Edmonton, Helena	Deduct 2 hours
Los Angeles, San Francisco, Reno, Portland, Seattle, Vancouver	Deduct 3 hours
Honolulu, Anchorage, Fairbanks, Kodiak	Deduct 5 hours
Nome, Samoa, Tonga, Midway	Deduct 6 hours
Halifax, Bermuda, San Juan, Caracas, La Paz, Barbados	Add 1 hour
St. John's, Brasilia, Rio de Janeiro, Sao Paulo, Buenos Aires, Montevideo	Add 2 hours
Azores, Cape Verde Islands	Add 3 hours
Canary Islands, Madeira, Reykjavik	Add 4 hours
London, Paris, Amsterdam, Madrid, Lisbon, Gibraltar, Belfast, Rabat	Add 5 hours
Frankfurt, Rome, Oslo, Stockholm, Prague, Belgrade	Add 6 hours
Bucharest, Beirut, Tel Aviv, Athens, Istanbul, Cairo, Alexandria, Cape Town, Johannesburg	Add 7 hours
Moscow, Leningrad, Baghdad, Dhahran, Addis Ababa, Nairobi, Teheran, Zanzibar	Add 8 hours
Bombay, Calcutta, Sri Lanka	Add 10½ hours
Hong Kong, Shanghai, Manila, Peking, Perth	Add 13 hours
Tokyo, Okinawa, Darwin, Pusan	Add 14 hours
Sydney, Melbourne, Port Moresby, Guam	Add 15 hours
Auckland, Wellington, Suva, Wake	Add 17 hours

1993 MOON TABLES—NEW YORK TIME

JANUARY
Day Moon Enters
1. Aries
2. Taurus 0:30 pm
3. Taurus
4. Gemini 8:42 pm
5. Gemini
6. Gemini
7. Cancer 1:10 am
8. Cancer
9. Leo 2:49 am
10. Leo
11. Virgo 3:20 pm
12. Virgo
13. Libra 4:30 am
14. Libra
15. Scorpio 7:42 am
16. Scorpio
17. Sagitt. 1:30 pm
18. Sagitt.
19. Capric. 9:46 pm
20. Capric.
21. Capric.
22. Aquar. 8:00 am
23. Aquar.
24. Pisces 7:47 pm
25. Pisces
26. Pisces
27. Aries 8:28 am
28. Aries
29. Taurus 8:37 pm
30. Taurus
31. Taurus

FEBRUARY
Day Moon Enters
1. Gemini 6:15 am
2. Gemini
3. Cancer 11:56 am
4. Cancer
5. Leo 1:51 pm
6. Leo
7. Virgo 1:29 pm
8. Virgo
9. Libra 12:58 pm
10. Libra
11. Scorpio 2:24 pm
12. Scorpio
13. Sagitt. 7:08 pm
14. Sagitt.
15. Sagitt.
16. Capric. 3:20 am
17. Capric.
18. Aquar. 2:05 pm
19. Aquar.
20. Aquar.
21. Pisces 5:12 am
22. Pisces
23. Aries 2:50 pm
24. Aries
25. Aries
26. Taurus 3:11 am
27. Taurus
28. Gemini 1:52 pm

MARCH
Day Moon Enters
1. Gemini
2. Cancer 9:16 pm
3. Cancer
4. Cancer
5. Leo 0:40 am
6. Leo
7. Virgo 0:52 am
8. Libra 11:46 pm
9. Libra 9:42 am
10. Scorpio 11:40 pm
11. Scorpio
12. Scorpio
13. Sagitt. 2:33 am
14. Sagitt.
15. Capric. 9:28 am
16. Capric.
17. Aquar. 7:52 pm
18. Aquar.
19. Aquar.
20. Pisces 8:11 am
21. Pisces
22. Aries 8:51 pm
23. Aries
24. Aries
25. Taurus 8:59 am
26. Taurus
27. Gemini 7:48 pm
28. Gemini
29. Gemini
30. Cancer 4:14 am
31. Cancer

Summer time to be considered where applicable.

1993 MOON TABLES—NEW YORK TIME

APRIL
Day Moon Enters
1. Leo 9:21 am
2. Leo
3. Virgo 11:10 am
4. Virgo
5. Libra 10:54 am
6. Libra
7. Scorpio 10:32 am
8. Scorpio
9. Sagitt. 1:10 pm
10. Sagitt.
11. Capric. 5:24 pm
12. Capric.
13. Capric.
14. Aquar. 2:36 am
15. Aquar.
16. Pisces 2:33 pm
17. Pisces
18. Pisces
19. Aries 3:14 am
20. Aries
21. Taurus 3:08 pm
22. Taurus
23. Taurus
24. Gemini 1:27 am
25. Gemini
26. Cancer 9:25 am
27. Cancer
28. Leo 3:39 pm
29. Leo
30. Virgo 7:00 pm

MAY
Day Moon Enters
1. Virgo
2. Libra 8:20 pm
3. Libra
4. Scorpio 8:57 pm
5. Scorpio
6. Sagitt. 10:35 pm
7. Sagitt.
8. Sagitt.
9. Capric. 2:51 am
10. Capric.
11. Aquar. 10:44 am
12. Aquar.
13. Pisces 9:51 pm
14. Pisces
15. Pisces
16. Aries 10:24 am
17. Aries
18. Taurus 10:16 pm
19. Taurus
20. Taurus
21. Gemini 8:07 am
22. Gemini
23. Cancer 3:38 pm
24. Cancer
25. Leo 9:03 pm
26. Leo
27. Leo
28. Virgo 0.46 am
29. Virgo
30. Libra 5:18 am
31. Libra

JUNE
Day Moon Enters
1. Scorpio 5:22 am
2. Scorpio
3. Sagitt. 8:01 am
4. Sagitt.
5. Capric. 12:26 pm
6. Capric.
7. Aquar. 7:39 pm
8. Aquar.
9. Aquar.
10. Pisces 5:57 am
11. Pisces
12. Aries 6:14 pm
13. Aries
14. Aries
15. Taurus 6:19 am
16. Taurus
17. Gemini 4:12 pm
18. Gemini
19. Cancer 11:05 pm
20. Cancer
21. Cancer
22. Leo 3:26 am
23. Leo
24. Virgo 6:18 am
25. Virgo
26. Libra 8:46 am
27. Libra
28. Scorpio 11:37 am
29. Scorpio
30. Sagitt. 3:28 pm

Summer time to be considered where applicable.

1993 MOON TABLES—NEW YORK TIME

JULY
Day Moon Enters
1. Sagitt.
2. Capric. 8:48 pm
3. Capric.
4. Capric.
5. Aquar. 4:14 am
6. Aquar.
7. Pisces 2:10 pm
8. Pisces
9. Pisces
10. Aries 2:11 am
11. Aries
12. Taurus 2:37 pm
13. Taurus
14. Taurus
15. Gemini 1:07 am
16. Gemini
17. Cancer 8:08 am
18. Cancer
19. Leo 11:47 am
20. Leo
21. Virgo 1:24 pm
22. Virgo
23. Libra 2:39 am
24. Libra
25. Scorpio 5:00 pm
26. Scorpio
27. Sagitt. 9:13 pm
28. Sagitt.
29. Sagitt.
30. Capric. 3:27 am
31. Capric.

AUGUST
Day Moon Enters
1. Aquar. 11:36 am
2. Aquar.
3. Pisces 9:44 pm
4. Pisces
5. Pisces
6. Aries 9:39 am
7. Aries
8. Taurus 10:22 pm
9. Taurus
10. Taurus
11. Gemini 9:47 am
12. Gemini
13. Cancer 5:46 pm
14. Cancer
15. Leo 9:43 pm
16. Leo
17. Virgo 10:41 pm
18. Virgo
19. Libra 10:35 pm
20. Libra
21. Scorpio 11:27 pm
22. Scorpio
23. Scorpio
24. Sagitt. 2:45 am
25. Sagitt.
26. Capric. 8:58 am
27. Capric.
28. Aquar. 5:42 pm
29. Aquar.
30. Aquar.
31. Pisces 4:19 am

SEPTEMBER
Day Moon Enters
1. Pisces
2. Aries 4:21 pm
3. Aries
4. Aries
5. Taurus 5:09 am
6. Taurus
7. Gemini 5:16 pm
8. Gemini
9. Gemini
10. Cancer 2:37 am
11. Cancer
12. Leo 7:51 am
13. Leo
14. Virgo 9:20 am
15. Virgo
16. Libra 8:44 am
17. Libra
18. Scorpio 8:15 am
19. Scorpio
20. Sagitt. 9:53 am
21. Sagitt.
22. Capric. 2:54 pm
23. Capric.
24. Aquar. 11:19 pm
25. Aquar.
26. Aquar.
27. Pisces 10:13 am
28. Pisces
29. Aries 10:29 pm
30. Aries

Summer time to be considered where applicable.

1993 MOON TABLES—NEW YORK TIME

OCTOBER
Day Moon Enters
1. Aries
2. Taurus 11:13 am
3. Taurus
4. Gemini 11:27 pm
5. Gemini
6. Gemini
7. Cancer 9:42 am
8. Cancer
9. Leo 4:34 pm
10. Leo
11. Virgo 7:36 pm
12. Virgo
13. Libra 7:47 pm
14. Libra
15. Scorpio 7:01 pm
16. Scorpio
17. Sagitt. 7:23 pm
18. Sagitt.
19. Capric. 10:42 pm
20. Capric.
21. Capric
22. Aquar. 5:49 am
23. Aquar.
24. Pisces 4:17 pm
25. Pisces
26. Pisces
27. Aries 4:39 am
28. Aries
29. Taurus 5:20 pm
30. Taurus
31. Taurus

NOVEMBER
Day Moon Enters
1. Gemini 5:13 am
2. Gemini
3. Cancer 3:25 pm
4. Cancer
5. Leo 11:06 pm
6. Leo
7. Leo
8. Virgo 3:47 am
9. Virgo
10. Libra 5:42 pm
11. Libra
12. Scorpio 6:00 am
13. Scorpio
14. Sagitt. 6:20 am
15. Sagitt.
16. Capric. 8:34 am
17. Capric.
18. Aquar. 2:08 pm
19. Aquar.
20. Pisces 11:27 pm
21. Pisces
22. Pisces
23. Aries 11:30 am
24. Aries
25. Aries
26. Taurus 0.14 am
27. Taurus
28. Gemini 11:48 am
29. Gemini
30. Cancer 9:17 pm

DECEMBER
Day Moon Enters
1. Cancer
2. Cancer
3. Leo 4:33 am
4. Leo
5. Virgo 9:43 am
6. Virgo
7. Libra 1:03 pm
8. Libra
9. Scorpio 3:04 pm
10. Scorpio
11. Sagitt. 4:39 pm
12. Sagitt.
13. Capric. 7:06 pm
14. Capric.
15. Aquar. 11:51 pm
16. Aquar.
17. Aquar.
18. Pisces 7:59 am
19. Pisces
20. Aries 7:19 pm
21. Aries
22. Aries
23. Taurus 8:05 am
24. Taurus
25. Gemini 7:46 pm
26. Gemini
27. Gemini
28. Cancer 4:46 am
29. Cancer
30. Leo 10:59 am
31. Leo

Summer time to be considered where applicable.

MOON TABLES / 105

1993 PHASES OF THE MOON—NEW YORK TIME

New Moon	First Quarter	Full Moon	Last Quarter
(1992)	(1992)	Jan. 8	Jan. 14
Jan. 22	Jan. 30	Feb. 6	Feb. 13
Feb. 21	Mar. 1	Mar. 8	Mar. 14
Mar. 23	Mar. 30	Apr. 6	Apr. 13
Apr. 21	Apr. 29	May 5	May 13
May 21	May 28	June 4	June 12
June 19	June 26	July 3	July 11
July 19	July 25	Aug. 2	Aug. 10
Aug. 17	Aug. 24	Aug. 31	Sep. 9
Sep. 15	Sep. 22	Sep. 30	Oct. 8
Oct. 15	Oct. 22	Oct. 30	Nov. 7
Nov. 13	Nov. 20	Nov. 29	Dec. 6
Dec. 13	Dec. 22	Dec. 28	(1994)

Summer time to be considered where applicable.

1993 FISHING GUIDE

	Good	Best
January	4-6-13-14-19-23	8-16-26
February	4-5-13-21-28	2-10-12-22
March	4-5-12-13-21-22	1-3-10-24-31
April	6-15-18-19-27-28	1-7-9-25
May	6-15-21-24-25-31	3-12-16-22
June	3-8-11-12-21-22-29-30	2-4-13-20-26
July	5-8-9-19-27	4-18-24-26
August	6-14-15-20-21-23	2-5-10-22
September	2-11-12-17-20-28-29	1-4-16-19-25
October	4-9-17-26-28-31	2-6-8-15-25
November	5-12-13-23-28	1-4-14-22-26
December	3-11-20-25-29-30	2-10-13-19

1993 PLANTING GUIDE

	Aboveground Crops	Root Crops	Pruning	Weeds Pests
January	9-12-16-22-27	3-8-14-21	1-18-31	2-6-10-23
February	4-8-12-21-23	2-6-10-17	16-24-25	16-24-25
March	4-8-13-17-31	11-17-27	14-24-25	1-6-19
April	1-4-8-17	6-12-22	10-20-21	2-15-25
May	1-6-15-24-29	4-11-20-21	8-17-18	13-22-27
June	2-11-21-25	1-6-16-27	4-13-14	9-18-23
July	8-18-22-26	4-13-24-31	1-11-29	6-16-20
August	5-14-19-23	1-10-21-27	7-25-26	3-12-29
September	1-11-15-19	6-17-23-24	3-4-22	8-13-26
October	8-13-17-25	3-4-15-21	1-2-19-20	6-10-23
November	4-9-13-22	1-11-17-27	15-24-25	2-7-19-29
December	2-6-10-19-29	8-15-24-25	12-13-22-23	1-4-17-22

THE PLANETS AND THE SIGNS THEY RULE

The signs of the Zodiac are linked to the planets in the following way. Each sign is governed or ruled by one or more planets. No matter where the planets are located in the sky at any given moment, they still rule their respective signs. When they travel through the signs they rule, they have special dignity and their effects are stronger.

Following is a list of the planets and the signs they rule. After looking at the list, go back over the definitions of the planets and see if you can determine how the planet ruling *your* Sun sign has affected your life.

SIGNS	RULING PLANETS
Aries	Mars, Pluto
Taurus	Venus
Gemini	Mercury
Cancer	Moon
Leo	Sun
Virgo	Mercury
Libra	Venus
Scorpio	Mars, Pluto
Sagittarius	Jupiter
Capricorn	Saturn
Aquarius	Saturn, Uranus
Pisces	Jupiter, Neptune

FREE CHOICE AND
THE VALUE OF PREDICTIONS

Now that you've had a chance to become familiar with some basic astrological principles, it's time to turn our attention to the matter of predictions. That was our original question after all: Can astrology peer into the future? Well, astrological prognostication is an awe-inspiring art and requires deep philosophical consideration before it is to be undertaken. Not only are there many grids that must be laid one upon the other before such predictions can be made, but there are ethical issues that plague every student of the stars. How much can you really see? How much should you tell? What is the difference between valuable data and negative or harmful programing?

If an astrologer tells you only the good things, you'll have little confidence in the analysis when you are passing through crisis. On the other hand, if the astrologer is a prophet of doom who can see nothing but the dark clouds on the horizon, you will eventually have to reject astrology because you will come to associate it with the bad luck in your life.

Astrology itself is beyond any practitioner's capacity to grasp it all. Unrealistic utopianism or gloomy determinism reflect not the truth of astrology but the truth of the astrologer interpreting what he sees. In order to solve problems and make accurate predictions, you have to be *able* to look on the dark side of things without dwelling there. You have to be able to take a look at *all* the possibilities, all the possible meanings of a certain planetary influence without jumping to premature conclusions. Objective scanning and assessment take much practice and great skill.

No matter how skilled the astrologer is, he cannot assume the responsibility for your life. Only you can take that responsibility as your life unfolds. In a way, the predictions of this book are glancing ahead up the road, much the way a road map can indicate turns up ahead this way or that. You, however, are still driving the car.

What then is a horoscope? If it is a picture of you at your moment of birth, are you then frozen forever in time and space, unable to budge or deviate from the harsh, unyielding declarations of the stars? Not at all.

The universe is always in motion. Each moment follows the moment before it. As the present is the result of all past choices and action, so the future is the result of today's choices. But if we can go to a planetary calendar and see where planets will be located two years from now, then how can individual free choice exist? This is a question that has haunted authors and philosophers since the first thinkers recorded their thoughts. In the end, of course, we must all reason things out for ourselves and come to our own conclusions. It is easy to be impressed or influenced by people who seem to know a lot more than we do, but in reality we must all find codes of beliefs with which we are the most comfortable.

But if we can stretch our imaginations up, up above the line of time as it exists from one point to another, we can almost see past, present and future, all together. We can almost feel this vibrant thread of creative free choice that pushes forward at every moment, actually causing the future to happen! Free will, that force that changes the entire course of a stream, exists within the substance of the stream of Mind itself. Past, present and future are mere stepping-stones across that great current.

Our lives continue a thread of an intelligent mind that existed before we were born and will exist after we die. It is like an endless relay race. At birth we pick up a torch and carry it, lighting the way through the darkness our whole lives with that miraculous light of consciousness of immortality, then we pass it on to others when we die. What we call the *unconscious* may be part of this great stream of Mind, which learns and shares experiences with everything that has ever lived or will ever live on this world or any other.

Yet we all come to Earth with different family circumstances, backgrounds and characteristics. We all come to life with different planetary configurations. Indeed each person *is* different, yet we are all the same. We have different tasks or responsibilities or life styles, but underneath we share a common current—the powerful stream of human intelligence. Each of us has different sets of circumstances to deal with because of the choices he or she has made in the past. We all possess different assets and have different resources to fall back on, weaknesses to strengthen and sides of our nature to transform. We are all what we are now because of what we were before. The present is the sum of the past. And we will be what we will be in the future because of what we are now. It's as simple as that.

It is foolish to pretend that there are no specific boundaries or limitations to any of our particular lives. Family background, racial, cultural or religious indoctrinations, physical characteristics, these are all inescapable facts of our being that must be incorporated and accepted into our maturing mind. But each person possesses the capacity for breakthrough, forgiveness and total transformation. It has taken millions of years since people first began to walk upright. We cannot expect an overnight evolution to take place. There are many things about our personalities that are very much like our parents. Sometimes that thought makes us uncomfortable, but it's true.

It's also true that we are not our parents. You are *you*, just you, and nobody else but you. That's one of the wondrous aspects of astrology. The levels on which each planetary configuration works out will vary from individual to individual. Often an aspect of selfishness will be manifested in one person, yet in another it may appear as sacrifice and kindness.

Development is inevitable in human consciousness. But the direction of that development is not. As plants

FREE CHOICE AND THE VALUE OF PREDICTIONS / 111

will bend toward the light as they grow, so there is the possibility for the human mind to grow toward the light of integrity and truth. The Age of Aquarius that everyone is talking about must first take place within each man's mind and heart. An era of peace, freedom and brotherhood cannot be legislated by any government, no matter how liberal. It has to be a spontaneous flow of human spirit and fellowship. It will be a magnificent dawning on the globe of consciousness that reflects the joy of the human heart to be part of the great stream of intelligence and love. It must be generated by an enlightened, realistic humanity. There's no law that can put it into effect, no magic potion to drink that will make it all come true. It will be the result of all people's efforts to assume their personal and social responsibilities and carve out a new destiny for humankind.

As you read the predictions in this book, bear in mind that they have been calculated by means of planetary positions for whole groups of people. Thus their value lies in your ability to coordinate what you read with the nature of your life's circumstances at the present time. You have seen how many complex relationships must be analyzed in individual horoscopes before sensible accurate conclusions can be drawn. No matter what the indications, a person has his or her own life, own intelligence, basic native strength that must ultimately be the source of action and purpose. When you are living truthfully and in harmony with what you know is right, there are no forces, threats or obstacles that can defeat you.

With these predictions, read the overall pattern and see how rhythms begin to emerge. They are not caused by remote alien forces, millions of miles out in space. You and the planets are one. What you do, they do. What they do, you do. But can you change their course? No, but you cannot change many of your basic characteristics either. Still, within that already existing framework, you are the master. You can still differentiate between what is right for you and what is not. You can seize opportunities and act on them, you can create beauty and seek love. The purpose of looking ahead is not to scare yourself out of your wits. Look ahead to enlarge your perspective, enhance your overall view of the life *you* are developing. Difficult periods cause stress certainly, but at the same time they give you the chance to reassess your condition, restate and redefine exactly what is important to you, so you can cherish your life more. Joyous periods should be lived to the fullest with the happiness and exuberance that each person richly deserves.

We are not living to fulfill any destiny prerecorded long ago. We are not here as punishment for some past, forgotten sin. We are here because we choose to be here and take part in the vast evolving mystery we call human intelligence.

Construct Your Own Horoscope Chart

The following pages will show you how you can draw up a simple chart for yourself, provided you know the time of your birth. If you do not have the exact time, but do know whether it was early morning, or about Noon or sometime in the afternoon or evening, pick an hour you think would be close. Work out your chart according to instructions. If your result turns out as totally different from your perception of *you*, try another hour; it might give a better character description.

Notes:
   (1) Symbols and descriptions of the Signs (p. 114) are found pages 54-65.
   (2) Symbols and descriptions of the Planets of the Solar System (p. 114) are found on pp. 83-91.
   (3) Detailed information re the Houses and their meanings are found on pages 80, 81 and 82.

**The Publishers Regret
That They Cannot Answer
Individuals' Questions.**

YOUR HOROSCOPE

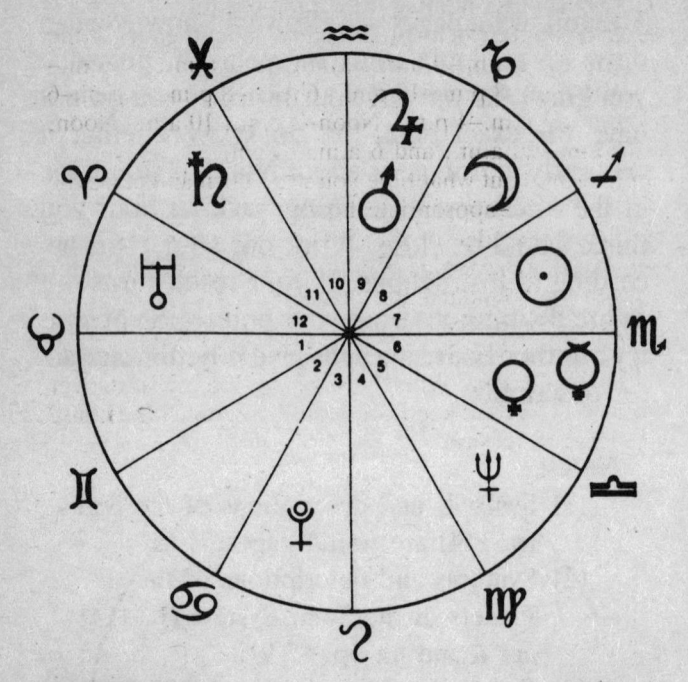

This person was born at 5:15 p.m. October 31 in New York City. The Sun is in Scorpio and is found in the 7th house. The Rising Sign, or the Sign governing house number 1, is Taurus, so this person is a blend of Scorpio and Taurus.

Construct Your Own Horoscope Chart:

1. Label house number 1: 4 a.m.–6 a.m.
2. In a counterclockwise direction, label the rest of the houses: 2 a.m.–4 a.m., Midnight–2.a.m., 10 p.m.–Midnight, 8 p.m.–10 p.m., 6 p.m.–8 p.m., 4 p.m.–6 p.m., 2 p.m.–4 p.m., Noon–2 p.m., 10 a.m.–Noon, 8 a.m.–10 a.m., and 6 a.m.–8 a.m.
3. Now find out what time you were born and place the Sun in the appropriate house.
4. Label the edge of that house with your Sun Sign. You now have a description of your basic character and your fundamental drives.
5. Label the rest of the houses with the Signs, starting with your Sun Sign, in order, still in a *counterclockwise direction*. When you get to Pisces, start over with Aries and keep going until you reach the house behind the Sun.

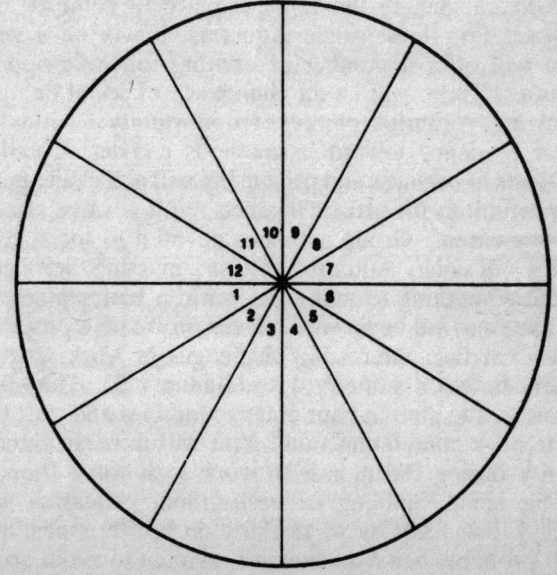

AQUARIUS
YEARLY FORECAST: 1993

*Forecast for 1993 Concerning Business
Prospects, Financial Affairs, Health,
Travel, Employment, Love and Marriage
for Persons Born with the Sun
in the Zodiacal Sign of Aquarius,
January 20–February 18.*

It will be a very interesting year for Aquarius with all indications pointing toward long-term growth. It will be a time when concentrated efforts will be devoted to the solidification of relationships, with particular emphasis placed on making the home a place of comfort and repose. For those single Aquarius, it will be a year that will offer a number of exciting romantic opportunities. There will be an abundance of social energy, allowing Aquarius plenty of opportunity to indulge their tendency toward harmonious contact. Creative projects in business and private life will add challenging opportunities for artistic instincts, with positive effects on the career. Group activities devoted to social concerns will satisfy Aquarius altruism, meeting their need to do something to make the world a better place.

The year will begin with a focus on creative projects. You will face interesting challenges at work, particularly between January 4 and January 22. They will allow you to stretch your creative muscles and start the year on a stimulating note. You will have an opportunity during the month to work with some friends, doing some building or restoration. Aquarius will spend time focusing particularly on health issues, and will probably begin an exercise regimen to avoid problems in the future. Later in the month there will be a tendency to be accident-prone so extra attention will be required to insure safety. The end of the month will be a time of high creativity and you will find yourself able to get much done at work with little effort.

February will begin with excellent communication and there will be exceptional ability to express ideas clearly, diminishing after the 8th when Mercury moves out of Aquarius. The month will see the realization of long-standing hopes related to a friendship possibility involving a secret affair. There will be continuing emphasis on exercise so spend some time outside in the country air, weather permitting. Later in the month there will be a growing concern with financial issues. Friends will stand with you in the time of need and you will feel bonds strengthening throughout the year. It will also be a good month for study and quiet pursuits. By joining a literary study group, you will satisfy your interest in working with groups, while studying at the same time.

March will find your attention drawn toward financial considerations, a timely development as tax season is here. Early in March you may have your home reappraised for insurance purposes. The month will not be good for secret affairs. If Aquarius is involved in any, there is strong likelihood of their becoming public knowledge between the 12th and 16th. It is not a good time, in general, for short, casual affairs. Movement after the 19th will be toward concentration on more serious matters. Altruistic feelings will grow strong and there will probably be some volunteer work with a political organization. Creative attention will be directed toward theater or participation in a drama group. Pure luck will be in Aquarius' favor for the second half of March and the early part of April.

Along with budding blossoms in April, Aquarius interests will expand, a development contributing to general improvements. This will be in the areas of personal finances sometime before the 12th of the month. Romantic affairs will also be more favorable than last month's. Overall the month will see good fortune in any endeavors to build or begin new projects. Aquarius will be very productive at work and will find that efforts to reach for new things will reap a harvest of benefits. Between April 5 and 12, it will be important to watch your nerves. After the 28th, disturbances that had troubled the family will evaporate and leave no residue.

The warmth of May will lead Aquarius toward a new interest, pursued in a formal course of study. A potential for boredom will exist if you leave yourself without a project to occupy your attention. You may well be involved in a writing project, anything from a major report for work to a play that has been germinating in your mind for some time. Writing will be most favorable between the 4th and the 19th. Whatever your new project, it will be one in which your family will be involved, offering more than just support and encouragement. The planets as well as the season will be favorable for romance. There may be some weekend trips during which it will blossom. Your confidence will be high throughout the month.

June will be a month for family reunions, celebrating a new undertaking, such as a marriage or a new home or both. Family will be the priority focus of your attention during the month and may be the source of some unlikely new romantic contacts. You will want to repay some debts to them and will be particularly extravagant in doing so. A reunion with some distant relative you haven't seen in some time will surprise you. The downside of the month will be volatile emotions, keeping you wary and perhaps a little unable to enjoy the prevailing good feelings.

July will be a time for romance and for nurturing new life. This could mean a baby for newlyweds or a new pet or garden for others, calling for tender loving care.

Those Aquarius owning a yard will spend much time landscaping. The land will be important for Aquarius throughout the month, and an opportunity may arise to join a partner in purchasing some land as a speculative venture. City dwellers will feel the need to escape and an extended vacation in the country will be enjoyed. An essential bond will have to be reinforced sometime during the month.

To Aquarius, August will not be the dog days, but will be a time of energy and activity. Work will involve you in many interesting and exciting projects, giving you much satisfaction. You will take an independent tack, either looking into the possibilities of self-employment or becoming involved in union activities. In any case, you will have plenty of energy left over and will gladly contribute it in service to others. Besides finding this endeavor very satisfying, you will also value it as a rewarding learning experience. Your art projects, be they writing, music or painting, will be the source of additional satisfaction. It will be a very full month.

September may be the month for marriage for single Aquarius. If not, a sound partnership could be formed, perhaps in a new business venture. Joint creative activities will be likely in the first half of the month. There may be sudden good news from legal sources, possibly of a small inheritance; be careful of the tax implications. The latter part of the month will see a cooling of relations outside of your primary partnership, probably spelling the end of many extramarital affairs. September will be a time when Aquarius will share the fruits of some of their educational ventures and will probably do some volunteer work related to teaching or tutoring.

During October, tax considerations that were indicated last month will become much more important. There will be contact with accountants that will be a nuisance, but will be necessary to protect financial resources. The positive factor throughout the month will

120 / YEARLY FORECAST—AQUARIUS

be harmonious relations with the opposite sex. This could mean another ideal opportunity for romance with a new partner entering the picture. Or the sudden ability to see the charms of your present partner with new eyes could rouse you. It will be a good period for study and research as earlier efforts will finally begin to pay some dividends.

Self-confidence will be high throughout November, and partly as a result, your career will be infused with new energy. Aquarius will then feel a new excitement and enthusiasm for the job. Leadership will be emphasized and considerable progress will be made toward career advancement. Despite continuing emphasis on the home throughout the year, Aquarius will be less of a homebody during November and will probably do some traveling. The trip might very well be a study tour. If an old friend is involved in this venture, some new affection will come to the surface in a surprising way. After the 11th there will be a general change in the way Aquarius views relationships.

The year will end much the same way it began, with good fortune smiling on Aquarius. The indications of positive career changes that became apparent in November will finally bear fruit in December. A promotion and change in career direction will probably be the result. Opportunities in all areas of life will open for Aquarius as the year winds down. The little troubles that sometimes bothered you will then be seen in perspective. Projects such as study, artistic endeavors or hobbies will be distinctly easier after December 8. Overseas travel might occur after the 15th and would be the most overt expression of the horizons opening before Aquarius. Health, self-confidence and relationships will all end the year on high notes.

AQUARIUS
DAILY FORECAST: 1993

1st Week/January 1–7

Friday January 1st is a good day to enjoy the holiday spirit with a few chosen friends. You feel positive about the coming year and are determined to make the most of its opportunities both in business and in projects related to personal growth. For the most part, your friends share your enthusiasm, but don't be discouraged by the subtle negativity of one of them.

Saturday the 2nd you want to tinker with machines or appliances, but feel it is a better time to complete a chore you want to get out of the way. Yesterday's social energies continue to prevail, but you feel practical. You might want to answer holiday greetings from distant friends, make some telephone calls or work on a project with your mate. Focus those energies.

Sunday the 3rd finds emotions are strong. Aquarius will defend personal opinions passionately, but there is some impulsiveness and a tendency to leap to conclusions. It is a day of strong intuition so that can lead to positive results. Events present you with new opportunities and excitement resulting in changes in existing relationships. It is a great time for romantic activities.

Monday the 4th finds you melancholy about the end of the holiday season, but positive energies continue to prevail, enabling you to regain your optimism. There is

122 / DAILY FORECAST—AQUARIUS

pressure at work to start tying up loose ends remaining from last year, such as writing reports or reorganizing procedures. The path ahead seems a little daunting causing a temporary wavering of resolve.

Tuesday the 5th is a very stimulating day that can get tense due to excessive excitement. Actions will be impulsive and you may be very emotional with a tendency to upset those around you. Seize any opportunity that arises to wield creative power for the good of others. Relationships can be strengthened by paying more attention to the thoughts behind them. Romantic contacts may appear unexpectedly.

Wednesday the 6th is a pleasant day, but be careful not to overindulge in rich food. There is an unfounded belief that others will do anything for you without your having to make a contribution or an effort. Try to avoid overspending as you are inclined to be very extravagant today. Romantic possibilities continue and you might get into deep discussions about the opposite sex.

Thursday the 7th has you feeling somewhat emotionally volatile, but your lover is very supportive and attentive to your needs. You are gaining momentum on your work projects and begin to think about some building or remodeling at home. Thoughts tend to lead to a reevaluation of financial considerations and a cautious approach is indicated. Consider any advice offered.

Weekly Summary

The year begins with a spirit of warmth and enthusiasm leading to a deeper appreciation of those whom you care about the most, whether they are around the corner or around the globe. You feel connected to them and use this to strengthen bonds that might not be quite as strong between you and others. You feel the importance of your position within your circle of friends and family. But this leads to your being a little careless and taking others for granted about midweek.

You are eager to get on with the year and feel that you will accomplish much. There is a period in which you put on the brakes and scale down your ambitions. Then you realize they are not unrealistic and again set your sights on achieving them. You may be a little intimidated by the coming weeks at work. There is much to accomplish in what seems like a little time, but you make a strong beginning toward your goal.

Because of your expansive mood, the romantic relationship you have is straightened out. If you are without romance, you begin to lay the groundwork for future possibilities and your prospects improve. You tend to feel very good about yourself now.

2nd Week/January 8–14

Friday the 8th proves you have had a busy week and feel a little worn out. But you are very thoughtful and your attention turns to philosophical subjects. You counter your tiredness by seeking stimulation and excitement and might get involved with an unusual crowd of people as a result. You can find a different kind of stimulation by working on plans you began earlier.

Saturday the 9th calls for caution. You might eat or drink too much today. You may find your mental and physical needs are in conflict. You feel the need to play, perhaps with a computer game or some other type of electronic equipment. At the same time, your attention begins to turn toward health considerations, perhaps an exercise program or the purchase of some exercise equipment. Get some ideas from friends.

124 / DAILY FORECAST—AQUARIUS

Sunday the 10th should find you approaching life in a passionate manner during this time. Try to avoid becoming obsessive about work. In close relationships, one partner might feel very restless, but will take time to try to find out why. Otherwise, it might get very confusing. Control your passion and use the day to reflect and learn so things will make more sense.

Monday the 11th brings another burst of energy to social life. Political questions will come to the forefront and you will want to make a contribution of money or time, even both. Aquarius will spend a great deal of time talking and arguing with friends so that passion might boil over, but there will be no harm done. Give some space to your mate and do not push for intimacy.

Tuesday the 12th will bring a pleasant sense of wellbeing. You feel warm and friendly toward people and want to do something to help others. Your emotions are under strict control and you take a sober and realistic view of life. You feel curiosity, but nonetheless take a businesslike approach to your tasks and toward people. You find this to be rewarding.

Wednesday the 13th finds deadlines beginning to loom ominously. But you also find that inventive friends help you to regain proper perspective on these and you again feel capable of getting the job done. You are a little irritable so think before you react. Because you are accident-prone, be careful in planning your adventures. Be sure to discuss plans with your mate.

Thursday the 14th has most people feeling very affectionate toward loved ones. Be careful, however, not to be overprotective. Think about yourself and your own needs. You will enjoy being surrounded by people who are connected with your past, perhaps old friends you haven't seen for a long time. But don't let nostalgia cause you to lose sight of the future. Beware of those who have ulterior motives.

Weekly Summary

This week you find yourself on a seesaw rocking back and forth between private concerns and social impulses. It may require a bit of struggle, but you eventually reach a harmonious balance between them. Work is something of a struggle because there is much to be done. Remember, however, you don't necessarily have to do it all yourself. This might be your opportunity to link personal concerns with those forces pulling you toward social interaction. You will be led to think of how your social energy can be better spent.

Don't allow your feelings toward people to lead you into taking for granted someone very close. As you spread your social energy around, the person closest to you may feel neglected. Save the most and best for that important person and your efforts will be rewarded. Initially you must remind yourself of their needs, but as the week passes your energies will naturally be focused in that direction.

There is a general restlessness that leads you to flit between different pastimes while remaining unable to focus on any one. Shape plans and formulate projects that will help you spend your solitary time.

3rd Week/January 15–21

Friday the 15th will find Aquarius to be a bit irritable. You may feel dissatisfied looking back at the week, considering what was accomplished and what was left undone. There is a tendency to be impulsive and escape from restrictions. It could be somewhat upsetting if you don't get your own way today. But although it might involve a struggle, you do get hold of your emotions.

Saturday the 16th is a very pleasant day. You return to the positive energy that has prevailed this month and are again able to relate well to people. Cast your concerns to the wind. It is a very good time for leisurely group activities. Your special group of friends will depend on your leadership, but don't be domineering. Make an effort to allow the group to set the pace collectively. You might even take a short trip.

Sunday the 17th will reveal your priorities may have to be changed, with a deemphasis on work and a greater focus on the home. Events can present you with opportunities for a broader range of emotional experience. An old relationship might be terminated, but a new one is likely to take its place, bringing with it fresh excitement that was lacking previously. Take advantage of this opportunity to make some graceful changes.

Monday the 18th is a good day for Aquarius to get a lot of work completed, either alone or in the company of others. Contentment is most likely to come from a leadership role where your independent thinking will be valued. The tempo of social interchange will again be increased and a great deal of time will be spent talking to friends. Take note and listen to them.

Tuesday the 19th sees the tide turn so it is not a good day for getting much done. You feel dreamy and you might want to pay attention to where the dreams are leading. Water will play a part in the day's activity, perhaps in the form of travel by boat. Be careful you don't misread this tendency and drink too much alcohol. Relationships are unpredictable and stormy.

Wednesday the 20th may find you with houseguests. Whether or not they visit, relatives will contribute time or advice and will help quicken the escape from inertia. You feel introverted, but are open to suggestion from outside and are fortunate in that it will be helpful. Business takes a turn for the better. Someone admires you from afar. Be sensitive to this new presence.

Thursday the 21st reveals that Aquarius is ready to focus his thoughts to clarify plans that have been slowly taking shape. It is time to move forward. Share your energy with your mate or a close friend. Discuss what has been on your mind and it will become clearer to both of you. Communication is emphasized. Your financial situation is changeable.

Weekly Summary

A flurry of confusion mars the middle of the week, but you are able to escape it with the help of your friends or associates. It has been stressful, but you can see that work is progressing nicely and that you are in better shape than you had imagined yourself to be. You are appreciated by others, but for a period of time lose sight of this and are very hard on yourself. Plans begin to take a more tangible shape.

Relationships are important and you are the focus of attention from both friends and family. When you begin to feeling a little lonely and sorry for yourself, people will come to your rescue repeatedly this week. They do depend on you, but are willing to give you back something in return. Your efforts will thus be more than rewarded.

You are a little irritable, but take the time to ponder the situation so things are put back in perspective. It is a week of much give-and-take that at times seems counterproductive. But by week's end, you will have been able to realize how much more has actually been accomplished than you had thought.

4th Week/January 22–28

Friday the 22nd proves the unexpected is likely to happen and spontaneity is the order of the day. Don't straitjacket yourself with preconceptions, but rather allow things to present themselves to you in their natural order and at their normal pace. A reversal at work brings unexpected benefits; don't fight it. A short, unexpected trip is likely, and a telephone call from someone who has been absent too long will surprise you.

Saturday the 23rd will find Aquarius is to have dinner with friends, and grudges that have lingered long are forgotten. There is harmonious music in the air; perhaps you will listen to it together. Political involvement is discussed and a new commitment is made. You are glad that you are who you are, and you want others to feel the same way about themselves.

Sunday the 24th will be a day where the tendency is toward indulgence. There will be a prevailing feeling of great pleasure in being alive and a sense of satisfaction with oneself. The worst thing that could happen today is overeating or, if you are on a diet, falling off of it. It is not a good day for making important decisions and communication is not good.

Monday the 25th will not find you looking for a fight, but you won't let anyone take advantage of your good nature. You will defend your beliefs with passionate fervor. You crave some excitement and are looking for something that departs from the normal routine. It is a good time to make some constructive changes in your personal life. Romantic relationships suddenly grow.

Tuesday the 26th reveals Aquarius' attention will be directed toward taking care of joint possessions. Perhaps it is time to decide to have more control over something that you and someone else share ownership. Don't overspend or get into debt as this will cause you to come under someone else's control. You feel a strong desire for a change of scenery and it is indicated, maybe in the form of a new job or a move.

Wednesday the 27th finds health is a factor today, but nothing serious is indicated. Creative activity can be helpful to personal problems as well as to health. Maybe you need just to take it more slowly. Remember your plans to make changes. Be sure to keep your feet on the ground, but don't stop yourself from dreaming. You will be called upon to lend assistance.

Thursday the 28th is another day that is better for planning than for action, but the time is coming soon to make a move. People behind the scenes can make an important contribution and a surprise is in order. There is some tension between home and work so be careful where you focus your attention. Money can be the cause of lovers' quarrels and can come between you.

Weekly Summary

The early part of the week is one in which events happen that you don't anticipate, but they wind up working in your favor. Spontaneous energies are emphasized. These energies bring social contact where bygones become bygones. There is a reaffirmation of closeness where it seemed unlikely to happen. This feeling leads to self-indulgences without regrets.

There will be some conflict and differences of opinion, but you will stand your ground. This will cause you to take a second look at things and will lead to a desire to make some changes. Fervent energy is abounding; it will find its way into your romance and will give it a considerable charge. It is a quietly turbulent time and you are pulled in several directions at once.

You will become a little worn out by the turbulence that underlies the week's activities and it will lead you further along the path of change. Health becomes a factor as a result of the unsettled nature of the week, and could cause you to slow down a good deal. This could result in a positive resolution of problems. There will be some problem striking a balance between home and office, and financial considerations worry you.

5th Week/January 29–February 4

Friday the 29th may present Aquarius with the possibilities of finding different ways of looking at life. Existing relationships will change for the better, but new relationships are likely to begin that might put some strain on old ones. Take the opportunity to make any changes as gracefully as possible. This is an excellent day for matters concerned with domestic life.

Saturday the 30th is the time to continue working on the changes you have planned for the home. It is also a good day to do the repairs and cleaning you have been putting off. Your desire to do these chores at last is particularly strong right now. The day is likely to be very busy socially with lots of small talk and gossiping. There may be a good chance to work on strengthening rapport with large groups, perhaps with a club.

Sunday the 31st will represent a challenge to the usual structure of daily life. This might concern a change in relationships at home. Or an upset over business associations, not usually requiring much thought, may occur. Underlying tensions will be brought to the surface.

You may be less tolerant of the opposite sex, so getting along with them will not be easy at the moment.

Monday February 1st brings a feeling of exuberance to go with the continued high energy that you have felt over the weekend. Along with this comes an inclination to take risks and maybe to be overconfident. These can be overcome by tapping into the tendency toward relaxation and taking things easy. There will be almost perfect balance between these inclinations.

Tuesday the 2nd will promote emotional power struggles with friends or associates. Aquarius will wind up either as the inciter or the victim of these struggles. It is best to keep a cool, detached demeanor and try to minimize the impact of these conflicts. The possible results could be a sense of guilt or jealousy, or the outcome could be positive for the future.

Wednesday the 3rd finds relations in general are greatly improved as Aquarius lowers defenses and allows others to get closer. Emotions will be felt in a deeper way, and protective and nurturing instincts will come to the fore. Involvement with children is likely, but try to suppress the tendency to be overprotective. Make a serious effort not to be too possessive or selfish.

Thursday the 4th reveals social energies abounding; it is a good day to be with friends. There is a strong feeling of love and friendship which will enrich and reward life right now. This feeling will aid and improve all love relationships as the existing rapport is as close to perfect as it can be. Home energies are also strong so it makes sense to combine these dominating forces.

Weekly Summary

The week finds Aquarius deeply involved in those social energies which are so much a part of their nature. Relationships change as new ones are created. The social impulse is also directed toward formal organizations and leadership qualities are emphasized.

There is a lot of motivation and much is completed that had being lying half-finished for some time. The home is in flux, partly because of your own efforts to make changes, and also due to an underlying current of change taking place. Be careful of this; pay attention and it will work out positively. The high spirits that are rampant will lead to dangerous overconfidence, but that will be counterbalanced by placid energies.

As the week progresses conflict will develop which will engulf Aquarius. By keeping perspective, however, damage will be avoided and the conflict could even prove advantageous. Later in the week, things will quiet down and the excitement will be replaced by a warm closeness, particularly with a child. Everything will culminate in a congenial gathering that will affirm both friendships and the home.

6th Week/February 5–11

Friday the 5th is a day when it becomes easier to deal with emotional issues. Aquarius maintains the stability that arose at the end of the previous week, and there is discipline and self-control now. Along with this comes a careful approach to work and a thrifty approach to finances. This mood brings a preference for the company of older, more serious people. Make the most of it.

Saturday the 6th finds romantic relationships tense due to a conflict between the desire to be close and the need to be free. Minimize this with a conscious effort to give loved ones the freedom you would desire for yourself. Also direct your focus toward those higher values represented by religion or philosophy. It is a favorable day and you feel positive and optimistic.

Sunday the 7th is a good day to devote some time to financial considerations. A short trip to an interesting spot can have favorable results, particularly for the children. Influential people or close associates can have a particularly beneficial effect on creative projects. It is a good day for negotiating informally with in-laws and settling some long-standing disagreements.

Monday the 8th will be a slow day, and thinking processes are more sluggish than they have been. There will be confusion concerning future plans and uncertainty about immediate tasks at hand. Clarity will come later in the day. Big decisions are not recommended, but don't allow everything to come to a standstill. Secret hopes for new friendships will bear fruit.

Tuesday the 9th is a quiet day and Aquarius must use tact with partners or close associates. Promised financial assistance becomes touchy due to unexpected differences between the parties involved. It is not a good day for dealing with banks or brokers as financial people can be difficult today. Take solace with loved ones as good relations with them are indicated.

Wednesday the 10th finds Aquarius smoothing out bumps in the road. It is a good time to make that move related to business. Financial affairs will take a turn for the better. Avoid being predictable today and much can be accomplished. Loved ones are very helpful and it's a good time to reward them. A small gift or dinner at a favorite restaurant would go a long way toward making them feel appreciated.

Thursday the 11th is complicated by personal health problems that can interfere with work or cause things to fall behind schedule. Your emotional well-being can be upset by worrying about things that are out of your control. Be careful not to do too much or you may find yourself unable to get anything done. Moderation is indicated. An animal is a calming factor.

Weekly Summary

The week begins with a sense of calm seriousness that is advantageous and very productive. Emotional stability has returned after a period of frantic excitability. This stability might lead to an apprehension that one is not being adventurous enough and that romantic closeness is beginning to feel confining. You can counter this by allowing others the freedom you feel you need and harmony will be regained. Along with this contentedness will come an interest in philosophical questions.

Financial affairs will need some attention by midweek. A family outing will inject a lighter tone into the fabric of life. There will be some loss of intellectual clarity and thoughts may be a little muddled, but perseverance will allow you to pass through this temporary situation undamaged and perhaps with a new friend.

Later in the week interpersonal relationships are a bit bumpy. It is not a good time for involvement with professionals. This is reversed suddenly and things take a quick turn for the better. Pay attention to loved ones and show your appreciation for their continued support. Health factors may slow down forward momentum but you will keep a clear head.

7th Week/February 12–18

Friday the 12th you may hear from long-distance friends or relatives during the day. You are very nurturing and supportive and will make a loan of money or your car to a family member. Your love life is a matter of concern and you may be somewhat preoccupied. Don't let temporary moodiness interfere with friendships. Try something creative in the kitchen.

Saturday the 13th gives personal relationships a strong boost of power. It is a sentimental day and heartfelt communication that reinforces relationships is likely. Your sentiment will cause you to focus on social problems and what you can do about them. Be moderate and don't wallow in your feelings. Be careful about a tendency toward overeating or drinking.

Sunday the 14th encourages Aquarius toward compulsive behavior. It will be difficult to fend off sudden urges and impulses. Along with this tendency comes a proclivity for self-analysis. The way to resolve outstanding issues will become clear to you with a little thought. It is also a good time to share your insightfulness with others. Join in some quiet discussions.

Monday the 15th is a restless time. You want to seek excitement but don't want to risk disruption of your life. You want to stimulate your companions and seek to do so without causing trouble. At home and in other close situations, you are not willing to accept the status quo. There is a strong possibility of travel, perhaps by airplane, indicated now and over the next few days.

Tuesday the 16th is a more controlled day. A sober and realistic point of view will lead you toward positive accomplishments. Common sense will prevail and you can overcome any problem or difficulty that may arise. There is a strong feeling of security and self-confidence in everything you undertake today. A period set aside for serious introspection would be very productive.

Wednesday the 17th merits a very careful and thorough approach to any work or activity. Tasks completed today will probably not need further attention later. Your emotional needs and your sense of responsibility are in balance. Care and thriftiness will prevail, and the overall mood will be serious but not dour. A soothing sense of quiet satisfaction will surround you today.

Thursday the 18th is a day of high productivity when working with others. Leadership and initiative are very strong at the moment. Be mindful in demonstrating independence so as not to disrupt the group. You are willing to take on challenges and will readily defend your point of view. Communication will be direct and there will be an attraction toward strong people.

Weekly Summary

Early in the week you will be preoccupied with family and friends and will demonstrate your feelings by an act of generosity. This preoccupation will cause some moodiness, but activities, perhaps in the kitchen, will help you to overcome it. Overnight this moodiness will be transformed into a tendency toward excessive sentimentality, but instead of getting bogged down, your attention will be turned toward concerns greater than your own private worries.

By the end of the weekend, you will become a bit obsessive, but focused thought and discussion will prevent you from losing yourself in idiosyncratic matters. You will want to make some changes and will find ways to alter normal patterns enough to inject some novelty into your life. Stability and a sense of calm will return as the workweek progresses.

Mental sharpness will be heightened as the end of the week approaches. You will be very productive, secure in your relationships, and will find it very easy to share thoughts and ideas with associates and loved ones. Your leadership will be valued and you will be appreciated for those things that you do so well.

8th Week/February 19–25

Friday the 19th should be a very energetic and active day, and the tempo of social activities will greatly increase. Mental acuity will peak, and Aquarius will spend a great deal of time communicating with others. Good spirits will reign and there will be a strong desire to spread them around as liberally as possible. It is also a time to let loved ones know you care deeply.

Saturday the 20th continues your good interpersonal skills and mental clarity; it is a very favorable time to write letters. News from distant friends is likely. It's still a good time to enjoy being with people and getting to know them better. This affectionate mood will encourage you to share old memories and reminisce. There will be a slight tendency to overindulge yourself.

Sunday the 21st is a good day for Aquarius to enjoy some exercise in the country air. Outdoor activity will be a good way to be with friends for more than strolling down memory lane. The evening is a good time for paying bills, organizing finances or making plans for the spring. Quiet pursuits such as reading or a romantic evening at home will make the most of the day's mood.

Monday the 22nd might start with a rather tense mood. In contrast to the spirit of the past few days, you may find it difficult to handle other people, but this will be of brief duration. One challenge will be to diffuse unpleasant situations without creating general havoc. Avoid defensiveness and don't take things personally. Self-assurance will help you weather storms and make the most of a bad situation. Be comforted by a friend.

Tuesday the 23rd will be a day for tender emotions and a vibrant closeness with your mate or closest friend. Aquarius will take a very realistic view of life that makes any strain or adversity easier to bear. There is an inclination toward patience and an opportunity to demonstrate strength of character. Older people will be a good source of advice should problems arise.

Wednesday the 24th calls for mindfulness since there is a tendency to be excitable and impulsive today. Changes may be called for in your immediate personal life. These changes should not be major ones, however, but should be very constructive. Pay attention to finances because there may be minor difficulties brewing that will become apparent in the near future.

Thursday the 25th is a day for favorable progress in business. You might take someone to dinner in a fancy restaurant to benefit your future. Agreements made with friends will have a positive influence in business or at home. Never rely on secrecy; it's better to discuss plans with an empathetic ally. Influential people will support you in a subtle yet reassuring way.

Weekly Summary

The week begins on an energy crest and you can take fullest advantage of this with much talking, sharing and camaraderie. Mental processes will be peaking and you should use every hour wisely. Be careful of overindulgence but if this is successfully avoided, much will be accomplished both in your personal relationships and in taking care of overdue chores and obligations.

There is a temporary loss of good spirits as the workweek begins, but things get back on track rather quickly. They don't, however, quite regain the level of energy felt over the weekend. Touchiness will be accentuated but there is no need to be defensive. Feelings of warmth will be restored but without the excessive social energy that characterized the weekend; it will be more sharply focused on a particular friend or lover. This will anchor Aquarius' feet in the ground.

The end of the week brings a propensity for change and emphasis is placed on the home. Financial considerations begin to come into play to a greater extent than they have recently. The week ends with a positive turnabout in business affairs, and promises are made and accepted that become factors in the near future.

9th Week/February 26–March 4

Friday the 26th is a day calling for the cooperation of relatives or business associates in implementing important plans; perhaps needed money can be obtained. The evening offers an opportunity to garner support from influential people. Keep the day free from secret plans or behind-the-scenes maneuvering. The marital situation is even and past difficulties are forgotten.

Saturday the 27th is calm and relaxed. You feel very optimistic about the future and your homelife is falling into place. You feel a mood of generosity and want to show that feeling. Make a special effort and let someone know that they are important to you. Express your personality and emotions. It is a good time for further work on ongoing creative projects.

Sunday the 28th feels a little sluggish, but it is a day for good luck. There is someone, maybe a Taurus, who has

140 / DAILY FORECAST—AQUARIUS

caught your eye. Make an approach whether it be for friendship or romance. Don't worry about your usual impulsiveness because it will work in your favor. You might participate in group activities of an intellectual nature, perhaps a literary group.

Monday March 1st is a typical Monday. The day will begin with travel difficulties and lateness will be common. There is a tendency to get overstressed about situations beyond your control and to compensate with self-indulgence. Take things in stride and don't overreact. It's a good day to spend time by yourself and concentrate on reading, writing or research projects.

Tuesday the 2nd is a quiet and fairly unimportant day, but pay attention to home and family affairs. Carefully investigate any new propositions that are presented and don't move too quickly into new ventures. There will be a social event at your home but don't let someone's moodiness dampen the spirits of other guests. Make young people feel that they are contributing.

Wednesday the 3rd will be tedious and is not a good day to start new projects, but it will be free from lingering problems. Like yourself, associates and acquaintances are friendly but lack any energy or enthusiasm. If you are unattached, you may feel a little lonely today but new friends are likely to come your way and make you feel much better.

Thursday the 4th is a another day of little accomplishment. Friends may be demanding, and during the morning hours they probably won't be helpful with problems you have on your mind. Don't take any financial risks, but it's a good day to go shopping if you spend carefully. Correspondence or a short trip can be very helpful to renew your energy. A forgotten item brings relief when it turns up unexpectedly.

Weekly Summary

There are good relations early in the week and they will be a factor in financial considerations. There will be an active sense of happiness related to your matrimonial situation, but that could be troubled by unnecessary secrecy. The weekend will bring a calm contentedness and optimism about the future. You will be very expressive, so share this good feeling with others.

Energy will begin to dissipate and be replaced by sluggishness. It is relieved somewhat by your introduction to a new person who has romantic possibilities. Group involvement is likely to lead into the workweek. Lateness and travel difficulties begin the week and set a tone the lingers into midweek. Work is troublesome but private intellectual activity makes this more bearable. The home and family become priorities but you share them with others by hosting a gathering.

The lack of energy continues through the end of the week, and you may experience loneliness with your general enervation. You begin to return to your normal level of activity by shopping and by making an effort to contact distant friends, probably via letter. The week ends on the upswing with the unexpected reclamation of something believed to be long gone.

10th Week/March 5–11

Friday the 5th is a good day for serious discussions with close friends but avoid wasting time on unnecessary trivialities. There is an emphasis on group projects, and it is a excellent day for conferences or meetings. You feel rare personal energy and should be full of confidence, but beware of conceit. Relationships are intense and there is the lurking danger of overpossessiveness.

Saturday the 6th is a very stimulating time. You are inclined to act independently without consulting others. Understand your essential personal needs and plan intelligently to satisfy them. It is an excellent moment to begin new business ventures. Friends will be helpful and offer advice that bolsters your private thoughts.

Sunday the 7th finds Aquarius with a good perspective on emotions, so it's a good time for self-analysis. It is a propitious day to convey ideas to others. Communication is emphasized, but you will be more inclined to talk than to listen. Make the most of it because you have valuable concepts to share. Your heightened mental alertness makes it possible to work out difficulties.

Monday the 8th is a good day for Aquarius to consider personal relations, domestic life and family needs. Events will occur that bring these elements to the forefront. There is a strong desire to make changes, from trivial ones like rearranging the furniture to major ones like discussing a move. Relationships are harmonious, particularly with members of the opposite sex.

Tuesday the 9th is a good time to go out and socialize. Aquarius feels gregarious and derives great enjoyment from being with people. It is a good time to entertain at home or to start a project designed to make the home more attractive. A shopping expedition is likely, but don't spend more than you originally intended.

Wednesday the 10th brings a romantic and dreamy mood. Spend it wisely by passing time with a loved one. Spend time at home as domestic surroundings will appeal more than usual for the next several days. Use time with close relatives to smooth over some ruffled feathers. Travel is not recommended; revel in comforting domesticity with compatible young people.

Thursday the 11th continues your propensity for positive communication. Even routine conversations with friends are fruitful. It's a good day for traveling but be careful when plans are formulated. There is a stress on independence and personal freedom but don't ignore your links to people who are important to you. You feel very healthy and are inclined to be generous.

Weekly Summary

Communication is emphasized at the beginning of the week and a lot of important ground is covered and decisions made. There is much subtle effort devoted to relationships. Your energies then become focused on more personal needs and considerations. This is a very good time to make substantial progress toward positive objectives. This self-involvement brings insight that is useful as the tide turns again toward efficient communication. Ideas clarified during this process are shared and prove beneficial to others.

At the start of the workweek, focus returns to the home and attention will be paid to making changes in that environment. There is a positive inner ferment that brings about constructive developments in many areas. Your energy will not remain exclusively concentrated on the home, and socializing is again indicated toward the end of the week. This will at first involve a large group of people, but as time passes it will be narrowed down to center on that special someone.

The fluctuation between home and society will result in more enriching relationships with a sudden emphasis on getting away from home for a brief vacation. Good health and high spirits will round out the week.

144 / DAILY FORECAST—AQUARIUS

11th Week/March 12–18

Friday the 12th presents the possibility of an emotional power struggle occurring today. The tactics used by others in this dispute can be quite destructive. Close family members may be prone to game playing, perhaps leading to a significant change in domestic life. You might meet someone whom you find fascinating.

Saturday the 13th find Aquarius sensitive to feelings, both his own and those of others. An air of honesty prevails. Understanding will be enhanced by a much greater ability to listen. People will sense your openness and interest and will ask you to help them with their problems. All day you radiate good feelings and you demonstrate a definite ability to charm people.

Sunday the 14th illustrates why Aquarius should make an effort to steer clear of negative people; they will exhaust you. It is a good day to spend with close friends. The day will be colored by a pleasant feeling of restlessness. There is a strong chance of meeting exciting new people or of encountering an old friend not seen or heard from recently. Your high energy will be evident to all around you.

Monday the 15th brings an opportunity to make real progress. Domestic life brings rich emotional rewards. Existing relationships provide more satisfaction than they have before. These new feelings will prompt new discoveries about the self. Understanding will become deeper because it's based on unusually acute intuition as well as logic. Be gentle with very young children.

Tuesday the 16th reveals self-indulgence exerting its negative influence. You might experience this as a propensity toward overeating or overdrinking. You will be very demanding of other people but somewhat unwilling to offer anything in return. It is a good day to keep to yourself and avoid disrupting relationships with your counterproductive energy. Focus on your inner self.

Wednesday the 17th presents an Aquarius recharged in both mind and body and ready to jump back into the swing of things. The entire day feels like a continuing jolt of energy and vitality. Relationships will function more smoothly than usual, and the dichotomy between mind and emotion will nearly disappear. You are sensitive to people so group efforts could be productive.

Thursday the 18th is not a good time to spend money. Aquarius is not ready to make a prudent decision about real needs and might behave foolishly in this regard. The day is tinted by a strong attachment to material objects that are associated with the past. Careless spending may be a way to fight this attachment, so it's a good day to indulge in quiet contemplation instead.

Weekly Summary

The week will begin with a subtle turbulence affecting and unsettling relationships, but these energies are quickly reversed to be followed by serene harmony based on Aquarius' sensitivity and concern. You will be hard on yourself but it helps lead to this positive reversal. Toward the end of the weekend, you tend to be susceptible to negative influences. Share your need for excitement with close friends and an unexpected closeness will suddenly materialize.

Energies will then turn toward the home, bringing a new richness and warmth. When this is experienced to the fullest, it will bring new self-knowledge and satisfaction. Generosity and warmth can lead to self-indulgence and a squandering of positive feelings if you are not careful. Ride through the negativity.

Toward the end of the week, a burst of energy ends the blues and cuts through the indecision and uncertainty. Vitality and emotion come together harmoniously to bring thoughts and feelings once again into sync. Be careful about spending money at the end of the week. Go with the feeling of nostalgia.

12th Week/March 19–25

Friday the 19th finds secrets of the heart becoming known to others and causing difficulties. Emotions seem unsettled but it is nonetheless a good time for clear thinking. Energy is high and can be put to good use. Home beckons and new thresholds can be crossed. It is a good time to smooth over long-standing uncertainties and hidden conflicts.

Saturday the 20th is a good time for Aquarius to take the initiative. The capacity to work well, either alone or in a small group, is indicated. In conversation with others, be open and honest about your emotions. Your firmness is respected by other people and you make a difference in their lives. Other strong-willed people are attracted to you because you have so much to give.

Sunday the 21st is another good day for communication. Much headway will be made in those group projects in which you have been involved. Your buoyant mood infects others, and your ability to charm others is stronger than usual. A great deal of time will be spent talking today, and although the tempo of social activities will be frenzied, much will be accomplished.

Monday the 22nd finds Aquarius' emotions well under control with a very realistic outlook on life. The patience and strength to endure any hardship is with you. Movement is toward the past and there will be a strong inclination to use old answers to meet new uncertainties. This strategy might do at the job but it would be better to try something different at home.

Tuesday the 23rd is a very pleasant day filled with interesting social contacts. You enjoy being with other people and many opportunities arise to make new friends. There is a tendency to be overprotective of those closest to you, but this attention is unnecessary and may be misinterpreted as an infringement. Make a conscious effort not to be possessive and bask in the good feelings that prevail.

Wednesday the 24th represents another milestone in your attempt to discern the inner workings of the cosmos. Contemplation of the spiritual aspects of life is most appropriate. There will be a contrasting influence pulling you in the opposite direction, so you must choose the path most suited to your needs. Despite these conflicts you feel full of energy and very optimistic. Romantic possibilities are heightened.

Thursday the 25th highlights financial considerations related to the home. There may be an exchange of money related to insurance matters. It's a good time to reevaluate what is most important in your life. It might again be time to seek new answers to old questions and to make some important changes. The time is right for starting to do things differently.

Weekly Summary

As the week begins Aquarius can tackle problems as they arise because there will be a preponderance of good, useful energy on his side. Communication and leadership will be emphasized. Because you will be in touch with feelings and emotions, you can understand your own needs with a clarity and precision that will enable you to control your own destiny. It is a good time to give some serious thought to those areas of your life harboring important unanswered questions.

In the middle of the week there might be some adversity at work, but you will continue to have the wherewithal to deal with it without too much difficulty. Nostalgia will tend to make you more conservative than you need be. There will be a situation that needs attention at home, and it will be better to think creatively than to let your nostalgic mood shape your response. It's a good time to try something new.

Toward the end of the week, you will be drawn to consider spiritual rather than practical realities. You will not, however, entirely escape the nagging needs of the present. You will be full of life, and this energy will add spice to the romantic side of your life.

13th Week/March 26–April 1

Friday the 26th will put you in contact with influential people who may pull strings to smooth obstacles in your path. Close associates might resent your advantages and feel threatened. Take the time to be sure your goals are realistic ones. Be careful not to be overly judgmental of others. Make an extra effort to soothe hurt feelings. Be more easygoing with children.

Saturday the 27th is an active day for joint projects that will be helpful in alleviating ongoing business frustrations. There may be differences over something held in joint ownership, but this can be resolved. With a frank discussion, disagreements can be worked out to everyone's satisfaction. It's a good time to do research to back up your hunches with specific information.

Sunday the 28th is a slow day, but creative ventures can be helpful to personal problems or health. Luck is perched on your shoulder today, and personal endeavors can be more effective than ever. Something in the background is moving toward you and bringing success with it. Relationships are harmonious and satisfying.

Monday the 29th is a quiet, slow-paced day. Business matters are free from conflicts, and lingering resentments are forgotten. You are able to get along well with others and communication is enhanced. Your intuitive powers are remarkably keen, so it is a good time to follow your gut feelings. It can be very productive to pool talents and expertise; positive results are likely to follow although they won't be seen immediately.

Tuesday the 30th is a favorable day for negotiating financial agreements that have been on the back burner for some time. Make a change in your daily routine, and attempt to forge a connection between different aspects of your life. It is a good time to bring together business associates and those people closest to you in private life. A short trip will bring favorable results.

Wednesday the 31st is a good day to make a purchase that will enrich your home environment. Financial matters should be considered but your judgment and taste will be good. You are full of energy and ambition today and want to make your mark on the world. Some time should be devoted to spreading some of the sunshine you feel radiating from within.

Thursday April 1st continues the ebullient mood, and Aquarius is inclined to indulge in the joking tradition of the day. There is also an acute mental sharpness and the good judgment to clear away confusion and quickly get to the root of complex questions. It is a good time to make difficult decisions, and financial matters should be considered. It is time to address matters that you have been procrastinating about, perhaps income tax.

Weekly Summary

The week will begin with some positive career developments, but there will be some related interpersonal tension. Relationships both on the job and at home do not start out on a good foot and will need some attention from you to minimize difficulties. The early part of the week is not a good time for you to play hunches. Make sure you have all the facts before you make any important decisions. Harmonious relationships will be restored before any real damage is done.

The good luck you have had in your job will become a factor in other aspects of your life before the weekend is over. It will be a positive time with you feeling satisfied and relaxed. Those feelings will lead you back into the new workweek with an ability to take a leadership role that maximizes productivity. Intuitive abilities will come back stronger than ever and your instincts will be right on the mark.

The end of the week will find you functioning at high levels of intellectual and physical energy. It will be an optimum time to tackle the most difficult decisions or projects. Both business and romantic partners will depend on your leadership. Relationships will be vibrant.

14th Week/April 2–8

Friday the 2nd intensifies your emotions, but at the same time, you feel very sensitive yet content. You are in a serious mood and will be drawn toward strong, clear-thinking people. You are open and sincere and this enhances your romantic relationships. You will have a soulful conversation with someone of the opposite sex. Feelings and frustrations will flow freely and you will listen attentively. A new closeness arises.

Saturday the 3rd surrounds Aquarius with people he has strong ties to. An excursion or dinner with this close group is likely. Your inner voice will be very active today and will send you confusing messages, so it is not a good day to make decisions on important issues. Forget long-term considerations and enjoy the good feelings. A letter might bring exciting news.

Sunday the 4th is the day to address the inner confusion that was intermittently on your mind yesterday. It is a good day to analyze yourself and identify those troublesome areas in your life that may need attention. If you have neglected relationships because other things seemed more pressing, it's time to make amends. Positive change is indicated once you realize where.

Monday the 5th is another day of thoughtfulness and introspection but energy is nonetheless running high. A feeling of strength and fitness prevails. Aquarius is willing to take chances but wants to use today to consider options carefully before plunging into new endeavors wholeheartedly. Significant changes are likely in the future as a result of careful first steps taken today.

Tuesday the 6th Aquarius begins to feel more lighthearted and easygoing than in recent days. There is a sense of satisfaction with accomplishments and a willingness to share the good feelings. It is a good time for giving an unexpected gift to demonstrate affections. There will be new interests, either in a romance or membership in a new organization.

Wednesday the 7th calls for care in controlling obsessive behavior. There will be a loss of energy that you will struggle against, vainly trying to preserve the mood of the past few days. Remember that some things cannot be forced and must be taken in stride and that sometimes it is better to pay attention to what is right before your eyes. The unexpected figures on this day.

Thursday the 8th is somewhat difficult, but the need to communicate is strongly felt. Don't be afraid to confide in others about matters that seem strictly personal but be choosy. The right person could be very helpful. Emotions may tend to overwhelm the intellect, and there will be physical sluggishness. Others will ask your advice. Consider their feelings and be tactful but don't be afraid to say what you think.

Weekly Summary

Emotions will be running high at the beginning of the week and you feel very connected to the people in your life. Romantic activities will be intense and you find yourself drawing much closer to the other person in your life. If there is no one person, major influences are acting to insure that there soon is one.

Later in the weekend, you grow more reflective and might be troubled by some inner confusion. It is a good time for self-examination to determine if there are any areas of your life in need of change. You might not necessarily be able to pinpoint them immediately, but the time is right to give it some thought.

As the workweek beings, you continue to be very thoughtful but will be filled with energy and will be ready to implement some of your decisions. Interests will broaden in directions that might include a new romance. The danger at the end of the week is getting too caught up in new plans and becoming obsessive about them. There will be a loss of some of the energy that has been in your favor and this might cause you to feel listless in contrast to how you have been feeling.

15th Week/April 9–15

Friday the 9th inclines Aquarius to keep feelings and thoughts to himself. The mood is for isolation and independence and for focusing on your own concerns. It is a good time to catch up on projects that have fallen behind schedule at the home or office. Much can be accomplished since your detachment will prevent you from being waylaid by unexpected interruptions.

Saturday the 10th presents unusual and unexpected happenings to interrupt your plans, but don't allow them to upset you as it will be an exciting day. There might be an occasion for travel that places you in a fascinating new environment. Children and animals may be factors in the day's activities. Despite the bad start, you will finish with a refreshing closeness.

Sunday the 11th finds the home an important factor in your life today. Your mood will be influenced by the holiday, and the family will be part of things, either as guests or because they are on your mind. You will have some uncertainty about your affection for some of them. Business matters will come up in discussions and you will have new ideas about ongoing projects.

Monday the 12th is a good day to avoid rash and indulgent actions. Your irritability may create consternation and you will have to spend time soothing hurt feelings. A conscious effort to let off steam harmlessly is recommended. Quiet patience is in order as the bumpy road will be a short one. The tendency will be toward an excessive defensiveness and sensitivity.

Tuesday the 13th will once again see emotions under control. It is a good time for Aquarius to put the home in order as a practical approach to any kind of work or responsibility. There is harmony in family and personal relationships. It is a good time to deal with older people, both for your own and their sakes. Clear your psychic slate for the onslaught of productive activity.

Wednesday the 14th there will be a much greater desire than usual to take the initiative as confidence and courage make a heady comeback. Your self-assurance will be greatly respected by others. You will be invigorated by a healthy understanding of your own feelings and desires. Because you radiate strength and vitality, you will attract others with a positive outlook.

Thursday the 15th Aquarius' enthusiasm and energy will light up the room. There is an overpowering desire to take the helm in group situations, either at work or socially. Your speech is direct and forceful, and others will respect this and pay attention to your good ideas. You will accomplish a great deal and inspire others.

Weekly Summary

There will be a sudden flip-flop early in the week. In just one day you will go from being able to concentrate productively on solitary projects to being plagued by interruptions that prevent you from getting anything done. Although you may feel very annoyed during the day, the long-term outcome will be beneficial to ongoing relationships.

Midweek you will again be irritable and will probably find it hard to get along with others. Social energy will be at a low point. You want to be alone but will be forced to honor social obligations. It will be difficult, but you will have to make the most of it and try not to upset others by your general grouchiness.

The last few days of the week will find you back in the swing of things. You will reinforce emotional bonds and utilize the opportunity to refresh relationships and make amends for your recent mood. Self-confidence will be high as you approach the end of the week, a decisive turnaround from a few days ago. You will take an active leadership role at work. Your communicative and intellectual abilities will be peaking.

16th Week/April 16–22

Friday the 16th brings pleasant feelings between you and those around you. It is a good time to get a lot done early in the day. Later you will feel the loss of the high energy levels of the past few days, but don't let this be a cause of dissatisfaction. The evening will be best spent with friends, simply having a good time and enjoying uncomplicated good feelings.

Saturday the 17th will be a day of quiet pleasure and an amorous mood will prevail. Linger in bed, particularly if there is someone to linger with; you will relate well to the opposite sex. Enjoy the closeness but recognize that even the closest relationship needs room to breathe. Make an effort to avoid jealousy and possessiveness. There will be strong support from family members and home resonates in your heart with a warm glow.

Sunday the 18th is a good day for entertaining friends in your home. You feel light, cheerful and connected, and others will pick up the mood. Be careful not to take others for granted. There is a self-indulgent side to the day that can overshadow its positive aspects. Keep a balanced perspective. Pay attention to youngsters.

Monday the 19th brings frustration because the smooth and efficient communication of last week has been lost and you seem to be at odds with others. It is not a good day to settle arguments as neither side will be willing to give an inch. Home looms important in your thoughts, but attention must be paid to doing your job. Restore an effective balance between the two.

Tuesday the 20th will offer a test of Aquarius' ability to translate ideas into realities. Foundations must be built beneath castles in the air. Muster the energy to get the hard work done and the results will be favorable. There will be a tendency to take risks, particularly in financial dealings. Be wary of others who may try to take advantage of you. The first step toward building a better world must be taken at home.

Wednesday the 21st finds emotions and feelings playing a pivotal role in your life right now. Aquarius feels generous and wants to express it. Surprisingly, the tables might be turned and an unforeseen gift received. Long-dormant relationships may come to sudden new life, perhaps in the form of contact from a former romantic partner. Decide which attachments you want.

Thursday the 22nd shows domestic life to be the source of an upset. Suppressed tension may suddenly surface and demand to be addressed. A partner at home may demand a change or insist fine-tuning be done. An accident or maintenance around the house may necessitate repair or reconstruction. Although communication might not be optimal, it will avert new trouble.

Weekly Summary

Early last week it wouldn't have seemed possible, but this week begins with a clear mind, a sense of satisfaction at what has been achieved and, most importantly, the warm radiance of good feelings between you and the people in your life. There will be romance, friendship and a rich appreciation of others. This good aura will be coupled with a penchant for self-indulgence.

You might not want to go back to work as there will be a conflict between the demands of the workplace and the secure comfort of the home early in the week. You will be a bit cantankerous and may argue somewhat unreasonably. You idealism will face the challenge of practicality and you will successfully struggle to forge a real connection between the two. There will be a temptation to accept dubious risks, particularly those related to finances.

The last days of the week will find your good mood unmatched by that of your mate. You feel magnanimous and will probably give an impulsive gift, but nonetheless there will be unanticipated conflict at home. You will have to make a concerted effort to deflect possible misunderstandings.

17th Week/April 23–29

Friday the 23rd finds Aquarius ready to take advantage of opportunities for graceful changes in his or her personal life. Existing relationships need to accommodate new emotional experiences without a total disruption. Attitudes can be adjusted to see friendships in a new, clearer light. In all aspects of life, value can be found hidden in areas where it was least expected.

Saturday the 24th will be a day of quiet reflection. Aquarius will find it difficult to feel anger or resentment toward anyone. Feelings of friendliness and protectiveness are particularly strong. It will be a good day for spring cleaning or other projects around the home involving the family. Although there will be a temporary minor upset at midday, the day will pass harmoniously.

Sunday the 25th will seethe with passion and there is a good chance for encounters with others who are in the same mood. Don't let emotions rule your life at this point, but at the same time don't run away from them. Relationships will be enhanced by serious rather than superficial communication. This will provide a needed jolt of adrenaline to boost your energy level out of the doldrums you have been in lately.

Monday the 26th you will continue to experience life with greater emotional intensity than usual. Aquarius will seek out those who allow themselves to experience themselves vividly. Strong passions will surface easily, so try to be patient with others. It is good to have actions and emotions in harmony, but today you risk an excessive expression of anger.

Tuesday the 27th you can take pride in your talents and accomplishments and should focus on how to go about getting what you most desire. You will find satisfaction in relating to others; this also helps you to achieve your own goals. It's a good time to consider broadening your outlook by exploring new interests. Expect minor but surprising changes to occur at home.

Wednesday the 28th will be a day of conflicting influences that will pull you hither and yon. It is recommended that any kind of hasty action be avoided. Look before you leap. You will be exposed to radical ideas that may cause you to rethink parts of your life. Your common sense and self-confidence will guide you through this short, stormy period of uncertainty.

Thursday the 29th is a time of concentrated experience, most of which will be very productive. Aquarius wants to make life more emotionally satisfying. Effective and positive changes will occur among family members that will infuse relationships with a new richness. This is an excellent time to make improvements in all aspects of the personal environment.

Weekly Summary

Change is in the wind as the week begins. This will be positive and will not upset your abundant good spirits. Attention will be focused on the home, and existing bonds will be strengthened to a rich and satisfying degree. These feelings will undergo a transformation after some time, and they will manifest themselves with an intensity that will be electrifying. Be careful as the week progresses toward its midpoint that this roiling cauldron of emotion doesn't become chaos.

A greater thoughtfulness will be the way you naturally back off from this troublesome emotional volatility. This will also help bring you closer to the people who have been a bit alienated by the force of your spiritual state. You will be able to use this thoughtfulness to expand your horizons and involve yourself in new projects.

The end of the week will give you enough distance to consider your recent feelings more objectively. You will have the perspective to see where change is indicated and will be committed to instituting those changes. Because of your response others will feel close to you and appreciate your efforts on their behalf.

18th Week/April 30–May 6

Friday the 30th finds impulsiveness and brash initiative ascendant now. There is a lot of energy to utilize, but it should be concentrated on projects that are close to home. Existing relationships will be intense, and you will be in the mood for romance this evening. This will be an optimistic day crammed full of stimulating events. Studies and hobbies provide excitement.

Saturday May 1st is a positive day in which warm feelings for friends and associates will dominate. You are likely to attract people who share your happy and generous mood, but you will lend you support to anyone needing a helping hand. Use your energy to finish those pesky jobs you may have been putting off, but save time to just sit back and enjoy your good feelings.

Sunday the 2nd will see a reversal of the social energies that abounded yesterday, and your attention will be directed inward for introspection and self-criticism. This may bring up feelings of inferiority, but don't take this to heart since it's very likely exaggerated. You can counteract negative feelings by considering the things you have successfully accomplished.

Monday the 3rd Aquarius is likely to feel romantic, but it is a time to quietly express affection rather than indulge wild passion. The home will be a soothing tonic after the competitive stress of work. Self-indulgence is indicated. You have earned it but more satisfaction will be derived from sharing a quiet interlude, perhaps a romantic dinner at home, with that special person.

Tuesday the 4th is a good time to stretch your outlook and explore new interests. You can take pride in your achievements, but now you need to find more effective ways of attaining your goals. You will find satisfaction in relating to others, and this aids in meeting your objectives. This day of ferment will conclude with positive modification at home. Gently advise a teenager.

Wednesday the 5th will find you and your mate disagreeing about a career issue, which causes difficulty at home. The problem may be that neither of you is paying attention to the needs of the other. Make an effort to listen as well as getting your own point across. This is a good day to present a new idea to your co-workers. Be willing to admit you have been wrong.

Thursday the 6th you seem to be on an emotional roller coaster, and it will be hard to concentrate. Do not be oversensitive and make an effort to be patient with co-workers who appear out to get you. An inability to get much done in the face of an impending deadline creates extreme stress. Be careful as there is a tendency to run away from problems rather than face them.

Weekly Summary

You will be passionate and romantic as the week begins. The good feelings you are immersed in will be a steady source of energy enabling you to complete those nagging chores you have put off for so long. You will feel very stimulated and will attract people who want to share your vivacity and good humor. There may be a temporary loss of enthusiasm as you entertain some second thoughts about what you are doing. Clear-eyed reflection will get you through this period of self-doubt.

Midweek there will be a pleasant day entirely dominated by romance and amorous considerations. Make the most of it as it gives you the energy to pursue your ever-broadening interests.

Harmonious relations will end abruptly and a dispute mars the latter part of the week. You are excessively sensitive and this dispute makes it difficult to regain your emotional focus. As the week ends, your emotions are in a tumult that leaves you prone to the building pressure of the workplace. The week closes on a som-

162 / DAILY FORECAST—AQUARIUS

ber note since you feel too tired to face the sudden problems and want an expedient escape from them.

19th Week/May 7–13

Friday the 7th is a terrific day for romantic excitement. You don't want to make a quiet, subtle approach but rather are more inclined to a no-holds-barred expression of affection. Your partner will appreciate your honesty and is likely to get swept up in the passion of your feelings. You feel robustly healthy and should formulate an exercise plan to help you to maintain your high energy. Be careful of extravagant spending.

Saturday the 8th finds you in some difficulty due to an off-the-cuff commitment made in the recent past. Travel and talk on the telephone are indicated. Trouble is minimized by postponing other plans and concentrating on the issues at hand. Some residual resentment is probably inevitable but instead of fixating on it, take the time to count your blessings.

Sunday the 9th calls for getting out of the house, perhaps puttering in the yard or going to the park for a long relaxing stroll. Activities may involve casual friends with whom you might not feel completely at ease, but the time will be surprisingly pleasant. Dinner at a nice restaurant with the person closest to you would be a good way to end the day.

Monday the 10th you should try to be as productive as possible in the morning because the afternoon won't be conducive to getting much done. It is also advisable to avoid making decisions in the afternoon as your judgment will not be up to par. The mood later in the day may lead to overindulgence in food or drink. The evening will be better because your mate is amorous.

Tuesday the 11th you might meet someone from overseas who seems strangely familiar and is quite intellectually stimulating. High energy returns and you are very much on the ball. You should undertake an artistic project at home, perhaps a painting or outlining a writing project that has been on your mind for a while.

Wednesday the 12th you continue on a project requiring great concentration, and you again surprise yourself with your ability to make rapid headway. Religious questions intrigue you, and you may get into a debate with someone whose ideas are diametrically opposed to your own. Artistic pursuits are greatly favored for the time being, and both your insight and skill in conveying your ideas to others are heightened.

Thursday the 13th is fortunately not a Friday, but nonetheless you feel your luck changing for the worse. Nothing dramatic need be feared, but the auspicious boosts that kept coming your way the past few days will be absent. Your concentration will not be as acute and your diminished vitality may frustrate you. Someone will be aware of your mood and will offer you assistance. Accept their help. It will be very beneficial.

Weekly Summary

The week begins in a positive mode as romance again takes precedence in your life. Your forthright revelation of your feelings will yield interesting and exciting results. You feel robust and extravagant, but there will be a slight reversal since you must allocate some time to fulfill a prior obligation.

A relaxing day will be followed by a productive morning before another bout of listlessness overtakes you to preclude both accomplishment and analytical thinking. This is only a temporary lull, and your stamina will return in a flash, stimulated by a new acquaintance. You will have more than enough strength to meet the demands of work; if you devote your excess energy to a project at home, you will reap much personal satisfaction.

Vitality abounds as you approach the end of the week. You will immerse yourself in satisfying activities and will find that you have the Midas touch in whatever you attempt. You are contemplative but will not withdraw from others; instead you share your insight and enthusiasm with them.

20th Week/May 14–20

Friday the 14th sees your self-confidence on a roll. It is a good day to make that purchase you have been considering. The home will be the scene of a heartwarming reunion. It's a good time to reexamine ideas and outlooks you may have unquestioningly inherited from your parents. Old ways of thinking may not apply to the new situations you currently face. An unusual approach to an old dilemma might produce a valuable insight.

Saturday the 15th brings an unexpected event that ushers sweeping changes into your life. This kicks off a surge of romantic energy that infuses an old relationship with sudden new passion. Be receptive to surprises and don't rush to judgment. There may be a temporary falling-out with someone close to you over finances, but roll with the punches and don't burn your bridges.

Sunday the 16th promises intense and somewhat puzzling experiences. It is a good time to look inward, analyze your feelings, perhaps your dreams, and find the clues to end confusion. Emotions from the past will continue to surface, so it's best to discern their real significance. A repeat of past power struggles with a parent or an older relative might disrupt the day.

Monday the 17th will see calm and balance return. You demonstrate a careful and reasoned approach to any problem, project or activity. This bodes well for the coming workweek. Your behind-the-scenes efforts and the importance of your contribution will be recognized. The company of older and wiser friends will be preferred for their tranquil natures.

Tuesday the 18th finds Aquarius with a strong desire to seize the initiative and take responsibility for helping a group or committee find its way out of an impasse. Your capacity to vanquish adversity is remarkable. Use this strength to forge ahead with business-related projects or your own artistic endeavors. It's a good day to put something aside you may need in the near future.

Wednesday the 19th Aquarius should proceed with caution. There is a sense that change is in the air, and major decisions should be put off for a couple of days. Don't let things come to a complete standstill, however, because although they may be subtle, there are some positive influences affecting you today. Careful attention will permit you to have a satisfying day.

Thursday the 20th is a day of extreme mood swings, and you will be unable to focus on anything you try to do. You feel depressed and lethargic but you may get a burst of sudden energy and feel like the world is your oyster. Don't let these variances trouble you because you won't stay in any one of them too long. It's best to minimize tasks and ride through the day.

Weekly Summary

Self-confidence peaks as the week begins. You should use that to find a new way to overcome dependence and stand up for yourself. An old romance may bloom with a sudden burgeoning of passion that will be astounding. Don't let a financial dispute dampen good feelings.

As you move toward midweek, there may be some confusion related to an intense experience that will call for you to take time out for some serious self-examination. Dormant emotions might surface to disrupt the day, but this will be minor, and by the following day, peace and tranquillity will have been restored. Work goes very smoothly and you will be recognized for the quality of your efforts. This will give you a boost that allows you to take the initiative.

As the week ends the positive energy that has been influencing Aquarius ebbs. The mood will be changeable so there will be a loss of focus. Important decisions should not be attempted at the end of the week, but don't put everything on hold. Positive energy, although lessened and subtle, still remains and is available.

21st Week/May 21–27

Friday the 21st Aquarius' moods will begin to level out. Once again you feel a firm foundation beneath your feet. It's still not a favorable time to work on any task that needs concentration, but it is not necessary to write the whole day off. Do intuitive work such as a painting or a decorating project that has been put off. You will still be irritable, so it is best not to involve yourself in any touchy interpersonal situations.

Saturday the 22nd will be a more settled period, but strong emotions still provoke you to seek out intense experiences. You won't go looking for a fight, but the opportunity may arise for you to defend your beliefs and you will do so vehemently. Relationships will reflect this aspect of your life and be suffused with passion. In communicating with others, your responses tend to be heartfelt.

Sunday the 23rd is a day to be in familiar surroundings replete with creature comforts to finally regain your stability after some bad days. You will feel an aura of tranquillity augmented by lots of support from the family. It will be a day for retrenchment and attaining a new perspective. It is a good time to make some plans for the immediate future. Protect what you value most.

Monday the 24th begins a period of generosity and good feelings toward others. Relations are very good right now, particularly with members of your own sex. Dealing with large groups of people is favored as your leadership abilities are at a zenith. Because people seek you out, trivial conversation may be distracting.

Tuesday the 25th Aquarius will want to share good feelings with friends rather than concentrate on things that need to be done. Private life will be richer and more rewarding, and work will seem like an intrusion on this harmonious idyll. Love relationships will thrive as there is good rapport between you. Health will be unsettled due to lingering stress.

Wednesday the 26th is a dramatic reversal of yesterday and is optimal for accomplishing serious work. You have a strong capacity to work hard, either by yourself or with others, but beware of entanglement in unsavory office politics. It's a day to shy away from your usual leadership role because of personal projects that demand attention. Be sure to get adequate rest tonight.

Thursday the 27th is an excellent opportunity to make some changes in your personal life. This might entail buying new furniture or rearranging what you have but could involve a dramatic alteration in your relationship with your mate. It's a good time to get rid of old habits in a graceful way. It will be a day of keen intuition and sensitivity to other's emotional needs, so it is unlikely that you will cause anyone needless pain.

Weekly Summary

The week starts with some residual emotional instability, but the wildly varying moods gradually coalesce on a firmer foundation. Even so, a tendency toward excitability persists. It's a good time to take care of those necessary but essentially boring tasks you tend to avoid. There will be some conflicts early in the week as a result of your emotional volatility.

Toward the end of the weekend, you will develop the positive outlook you have been seeking. You feel content and in tune with the other people in your life. Love relations will be rewarding, and you have the drive and ambition to assume a leadership role at work. Because of the strength of relations in your private life, you may be a little impatient with the demands of work, but you will still be very productive.

Later in the week you again decline the leadership role because you want to direct your energy to the completion of ongoing projects. You end the week on an emotional high and you feel the strength of your intuition; this increased sensitivity causes you to relate well to others. This is an ideal time for making changes in your primary relationship.

22nd Week/May 28–June 3

Friday the 28th enables you to successfully complete whatever task is undertaken. It is an excellent day for doing those complex tasks that require intense concentration. There is a danger of ego conflicts since you attract others who are feeling equally empowered; power struggles may ensue. It's a good day to stand your ground but don't be unreasonable. There will be an overture of friendship from an unlikely source.

Saturday the 29th is a time for new discoveries. A sense of curiosity will prevail and new people will provide some sought-after stimulation. It's a favorable day to tackle unresolved conflicts that have simmered for too long. You will take a novel approach toward finding a solution and your efforts will be successful.

Sunday the 30th is a good day to relax and take it easy, perhaps by getting into the holiday spirit and having a picnic outdoors. Don't go far from home if you do, because you gain the maximum benefit through proximity to familiar surroundings. You feel very optimistic and generous. There is general harmony among family members, but a slight upset between you and the youngest member is likely. Don't dwell on it.

Monday the 31st you feel a burst of energy, and although you planned to relax, you resolve to do some work. A creative project demands attention, so you capitalize on your mood. The family feels somewhat neglected, and you have to endure many attempts to distract you. By midday, the time is right for you to share yourself with others, so make an extra effort.

Tuesday June 1st brings the ability to learn and rapidly assimilate new ideas. Your mind is logical and able to move from one subject to another without losing focus. There may be a conflict with a superior at work, but your dedication and insight are impressive. Steps will be taken that will advance your career. Financial matters will distract your attention during the workday.

170 / DAILY FORECAST—AQUARIUS

Wednesday the 2nd brings the risk of acting impulsively almost as a reaction to the careful thought you displayed yesterday. You will be somewhat fixated on exercising your will and getting your own way. Make an effort to calm down and be willing to compromise on certain issues that are not that important. Your mate may resent an oversight, and you will have to spend some time and perhaps money to make amends.

Thursday the 3rd has news from afar that helps you realize how important it is to occasionally reconsider priorities. There might be an imbalance in your life. Are you neglecting one area of responsibility in favor of another? You are motivated toward realizing ideals, but be careful not to neglect concerns closer to home. Communication needs to be improved as you have become distant from the people in your life.

Weekly Summary

As the week begins, you feel in total control of anything you attempt and you will be able to accomplish much. Because of your pride, there is a danger that egotism might create a conflict. You will be drawn to novelty. That makes you ready for new people who enter your life and open new horizons for exploration.

You will be very relaxed and ready to enjoy the holiday mood in the bosom of your family, but a sudden burst of intellectual energy leads you to a solitary undertaking as the weekend ends. You have the curiosity and presence of mind to assimilate new concepts and put them to productive use. Some of this healthy vitality should be devoted to financial issues.

Stubbornness and conceit may get in your way toward the end of the week, and you will lose some of the energy that has been giving you such a feeling of stability and power. You need to take stock of your situation to determine if you are maintaining a proper balance among the different areas of your life. Try not to favor one aspect at the expense of another. Be careful that you don't allow selfishness to interfere.

23rd Week/June 4–10

Friday the 4th Aquarius will be able to strike a balance between emotional needs and a sense of duty or obligation. Be careful to pay attention and take a thorough approach to any project or job you undertake. Your contented mood deepens from being with others. It is a good time for group efforts as they will benefit all involved. There may be a spark kindled between you and a new acquaintance met through a friend.

Saturday the 5th brings a strong urge to get away from the daily grind and go somewhere by yourself. Travel can be beneficial at this time, but the break from routine should not be too radical. It might be preferable to make a mental journey by immersing yourself in a creative project or registering for a course this summer. The evening will be an exciting one for romance.

Sunday the 6th may surprise you with a telephone call from a member of the extended family who informs you of an impending marriage. A get-together might be planned to give everyone an opportunity to discuss the matter further. There will be a decline in energy as the day wanes, but a prevailing closeness among members of the immediate family makes you appreciate the intimacy of the home. Final touches will be made to an assignment whose due date is nearing.

Monday the 7th sees issues related to both your domestic situation and your professional life brought into sharper focus. There may be confusion, but close interpersonal relationships continue to exert a warm and stabilizing influence. Communication with others might be unclear, so it's a good time for solitary efforts rather than working with others. Plan for the week ahead.

Tuesday the 8th Aquarius should be careful because there is a tendency to be overly excitable. It will be easy to leap to the wrong conclusion, especially about matters related to business. It is best to avoid making any irrevocable or decisive moves at this time. There is a good chance of meeting someone decidedly out of the ordinary who has definite romantic potential.

Wednesday the 9th isn't a day of great accomplishment. Your thoughts continually drift to the future, and daydreaming fritters away much of your time. Images derived from last night's dreams may preoccupy you for most of the morning. The imagination will be in overdrive for most of the day. If you are careful to separate fantasy from reality, this can be a useful period.

Thursday the 10th finds you incapable of feeling anger or resentment toward anyone. A deep-seated warmth permeates your psyche for the entire day. You are protective and desire to nurture those around you. When working with groups, your sympathetic and understanding attitude keeps things running smoothly. At home, an air of conviviality prevails.

Weekly Summary

Because you made the effort to correct an imbalance, this week starts with the different sides of your life in happy harmony. Your contentedness will help when you begin the week by meeting someone new and intriguing. Perhaps because of this, you may want to change your typical routine to allow for new experiences and might feel the need to travel. A mental rather than physical journey may be preferred. Over the weekend, romantic energies will be intense.

Restlessness will be the prevailing mood throughout the midweek period. You will be excitable and find it difficult to communicate. You may be both highstrung and impulsive, and your judgment will not be the best, so it will not be a good time for crucial decisions. Events and people at home exert stabilizing influences.

Your imagination will flare into sudden and intense activity at the end of the week. This helps get your mind off the confusion that has reigned in recent days and will aid as your mood stabilizes. Now you can return to the foundation furnished by those relationships from which you draw your primary strength.

24th Week/June 11–17

Friday the 11th is a time of equilibrium and harmony that rules all aspects of your life. The demands imposed on you from outside are exactly equal to your ability to meet them. A quiet and objective mental state casts everything in a favorable light. You should attempt to deal with thorny issues and make important decisions because you can now objectively weigh all options.

Saturday the 12th will be experienced with a strong emotional edge that makes you feel everything in an extremely acute manner. Although there won't be any overt conflicts, relationships will have an intensity that will give them an irresistibly exciting electricity. Your dealings with others will be frank and straightforward, and it's a good time to jointly plan for the future.

Sunday the 13th will bring displays of affection and love for those nearest you. It is an ideal day to spend with the people you feel closest to as there will be a marvelous opportunity to enrich these relationships and further strengthen existing bonds. The only negative aspect will be a predilection toward overindulgence that will ultimately deflate the upbeat mood.

Monday the 14th will begin with a continuation of yesterday's good vibrations until about midmorning. Your mood will begin to alter as the usual daily stress mounts and temporarily threatens to get out of control. The prevailing atmosphere, however, is favorable, and equilibrium will be restored after a brief period of emotional disarray. Relationships with most people will be very good for the rest of the day.

Tuesday the 15th is an optimal period for shifting your attention from domestic needs to the workplace. A little effort goes a long way toward securing your position and moving upward on the ladder of success. A break in a relationship that interferes with your ability to work on personal projects is likely to happen in the near future. You may lose one old friend but win a new one, and the balance will be in your favor.

Wednesday the 16th finds you insecure about certain things you have done at home. Be wary of people who are very demanding and threaten to distract you from what you know to be the best course of action. You should exert your dynamic personality to smooth over difficulties in the workplace. The same kind of leadership might be needed at home.

Thursday the 17th is a good day to start a project that will demand continuing discipline and willpower. Your efforts will lead to a resounding triumph. You may get word that someone is bad-mouthing you, so you should maintain good communications with both co-workers and superiors. Despite the undercurrent of mistrust at the office, tonight is perfect for romance at home.

Weekly Summary

You will coast through the early part of the week feeling that your life is under control. You derive a lot of satisfaction from the things you have and the achievements you have attained. Now you should set about making some vital decisions about the future, both alone and with your partner. You will feel a strong closeness to others through the first half of the week.

Stress mounts when you return to work, and this may temporarily undermine your continuing good spirits. You will soon be able to restore the positive outlook you have had in recent days. You now rise to meet challenges head-on and take steps that will ultimately enhance your future career prospects.

At the end of the week you will face obstacles at home and at work. You will be called upon to exercise your leadership abilities to bring a situation that is potentially very damaging under control. This same kind of forcefulness will be needed to avert a crisis at home as well. It will be important to focus some of your energy on preserving good communications, and as a reward, the week will end on a very romantic note.

25th Week/June 18–24

Friday the 18th finds concern for social and individual justice more pressing than usual. Emotions are strong and Aquarius feels in tune with the needs of others. It's a good day to participate in social organizations since your persuasive talents are peaking. Use them to illustrate the validity of your compassionate point of view. There will also be energy to lavish on relationships.

176 / DAILY FORECAST—AQUARIUS

Saturday the 19th calls for spending time with agreeable people. It is a great time for group activities, particularly those designed to benefit others. Altruism colors most events and Aquarius will feel a positive aura about life today. A pleasant surprise at home will add considerably to the overall good spirit.

Sunday the 20th will probably be a quiet time. You receive quiet enjoyment from playful pursuits in the morning, perhaps helping a child build something. It's time to pay back some long-term debts to your parents or to show your appreciation for a favor in the past. You should bestow an extravagance on your family to remind them how important they are to you.

Monday the 21st the mind and body will be well charged for the coming workweek. The day will be perceived as an unending burst of energy in which your emotions and physical vitality complement each other. Relations with members of the opposite sex are particularly harmonious. You will engender encouragement from an unexpected source. Bask in the good spirits.

Tuesday the 22nd will be a time of psychological perplexity and emotional turmoil. Some manifestations will be upsets, imprudent behavior and sudden mood shifts. Concentration is impossible so it is unlikely that you will accomplish much. There may be an alteration in relationships at home that might at first seem cataclysmic, but don't be too quick to make that judgment; things will regain their proper balance.

Wednesday the 23rd Aquarius has a tendency toward irritability and an inability to communicate effectively. Impatient behavior may erupt without warning; this expresses an underlying dissatisfaction that has its roots in lingering misgivings about ongoing relationships.

Long-buried tensions are likely to surface and demand attention, but confusion makes it difficult to do so.

Thursday the 24th will find subjective considerations still the primary focus of most mental processes. Aquarius will need to confirm his or her place in others' affections and to obtain reassurance that he or she is needed and appreciated. You may express your emotional needs by paying attention to others in an attempt to receive the same in return. The tide will begin to turn toward evening, and romance is in store.

Weekly Summary

Compassion and generosity are the qualities governing the first few days of the week. Aquarius will be very altruistic and will be concerned with finding ways to help others who don't have the advantages or even the necessities that most of us take for granted. This spirit will also be directed toward those most important in your life. Your selfless acts cause good fortune to return and a pleasant surprise to repay your kindness.

You will have ample energy available early in the workweek, fomenting high productivity and good relations, particularly with the opposite sex. Your mood will be lifted by a boost from a very unlikely source.

Unfortunately, there will be a turnaround as you get closer to the end of the week. Vitality will abate, making concentration that much more difficult. Because you will fight this change, you may become impulsive and moody and might bring your troubles home to upset the balance there. Your emotional poverty is in marked contrast to the abundance you felt earlier in the week; you may again be giving, not out of generosity but as a ploy to get what you need.

178 / DAILY FORECAST—AQUARIUS

26th Week/June 25–July 1

Friday the 25th finds relationships once again functioning on an optimal level. You want to spend time at home but will share it with close friends. You feel self-confident and your mood is light and cheerful. A very pleasant time is indicated; it is the perfect antidote to recent insecurity. Unusual opportunities loom in the evening hours and love relationships are favored.

Saturday the 26th is a quiet and independent time. Organizing thoughts and getting a fresh perspective would be fruitful pursuits. Don't be impatient about interruptions and try to be willing to give time and consideration to others. This is a good opportunity for closeness. The evening bodes well for an outing to a movie, play or dinner at a casual restaurant.

Sunday the 27th calls for the resolution of far-flung family conflicts since they will be visiting soon. Health problems may upset long-standing plans. You may enjoyably spend the day reminiscing with a loved one whom you haven't seen recently. It will take an effort, but you can avoid a disruption between you and your mate over your paying attention to someone else.

Monday the 28th sees your energies gradually building until a very high level is attained. Aquarius is ready, willing and able to work hard and you accomplish a great deal over the course of the day. There is a need to develop better harmony between home and work life, but don't let simmering conflicts related to this situation get out of hand. There may be a change of plans for the evening due to difficulties with transportation.

Tuesday the 29th is an emotionally controlled period since your different personality elements are well balanced and not fighting each other. It is a good time to concentrate on decisions, future plans and long-term projects. Because such levelheadedness dominates, you should spend time with people you like to see but sometimes avoid because of an occasional difficulty.

Wednesday the 30th gives a continuing sense of comfort and well-being. Aquarius will feel warm and friendly toward the people around him or her. People who also feel good will be attracted to you. There may be an encounter with a woman seeking emotional support and you readily give it. A token of appreciation may be received for a favor done and since forgotten.

Thursday July 1st will be the day vacation plans are finally confirmed after some indecision and much discussion. Family plays a role in the final outcome after a long-distance telephone conversation. Educational matters may interrupt the workday, probably related to enrolling in a training course to polish job-related skills. There will some tension with a co-worker and a tendency to hold a grudge.

Weekly Summary

As the week begins, you get what you need to restore your self-confidence and your optimism. The company of friends will make you feel important and loved and will present some interesting new romantic possibilities. Now with balance restored, you will again turn inward to give some quiet attention and consideration to the path your life is taking and what, if anything, needs to be done to improve it. Another casual gathering will capitalize on the social energies that abound.

A minor illness may disrupt plans but it won't prevent you from sharing some quality time with someone who has been absent. Due to jealousy, tensions with your mate might erupt into a minor squabble, but you have the wherewithal to avoid any major problems.

The second half of the week is filled with positive energy that exercises its influence without any major interference. You will be able to get a very satisfying and surprising amount of work done. Relations with people will be exceptional; there will be a unique clarity of thought and ability to make reasoned decisions.

27th Week/July 2–8

Friday the 2nd is a day when feelings and emotions play an important role. Relationships are quite good now, and a friendship that has been slowly growing for a long time is finally recognized as a close and rewarding one. You will probably be feeling self-indulgent and undisciplined, so don't expect to be able to get much serious work done. Don't allow impatience to mar the day.

Saturday the 3rd comes with strong desires that manifest themselves as a noticeable eagerness to give and receive love. Don't waste this opportunity to enjoy a satisfying time with your mate. If you are unattached, don't hesitate to go out on a limb with that person you have been quietly courting for some time. It's a good time to let him or her know how you really feel.

Sunday the 4th will be a day of reversal. You have a gathering planned and want to relax and enjoy the holiday, but confrontations with others are strongly indicated. Lovers especially may use various ploys to force each other to act in a certain way and communication will be strained. This can be avoided by anticipating the moves of those who are spoiling for a fight and short-circuiting them with acts of kindness.

Monday the 5th is the time to enjoy the untroubled fellowship that was threatened yesterday by the undercurrent of conflict. Today harmony and warm feelings prevail, although a short period of tension may disturb the early afternoon. The quiet of early evening when you finally get to be alone with the person most important to you is satisfying. Savor precious moments.

Tuesday the 6th will be a day of exceptional balance between your emotions and reason. You can empathize with great sensitivity but at the same time remain logical and precise in your thought processes. It's a perfect time to formulate a practical yet creative plan to achieve short-term goals that have previously eluded you. Communication with friends will be open and satisfying, so it is a good time to write letters.

Wednesday the 7th brings serious events, but these don't necessarily pose a problem because Aquarius will deal with them in a clearheaded and straightforward manner. There is no need to befuddle issues with fantasy, so be sure not to yield to that temptation. You feel assertive throughout the day, but this is tempered by a willingness to listen and to accept compromises.

Thursday the 8th will be a preference for serious people and an interest in conversation about important rather than frivolous subjects. You should take a careful approach to anything you do; patience and presence of mind will enable you to tackle any obstacle. It's a good time to use your wisdom to guide a younger person through a stressful time in his or her life.

Weekly Summary

The week will begin with a new friendship, evidence of the warm and openhearted emotions that characterize your psyche. You won't be able to get many practical tasks completed but should instead make the most of your feelings for the first couple of days. It is also a good time to take some romantic risks.

Toward the middle of the week, harmonious relations will come to an abrupt end and an undertone of mounting tensions disrupt the day. You can try to avoid conflict by going out of your way, and also against your inclinations, to be nice. A more sudden about-face than the one that occurs couldn't be imagined.

Relationships will glow with a new warmth and as the holiday ends, and there will be an exceptionally satisfying balance between feelings and ideas. Sensitivity to others will be very high, but there will also be a clearness of thought that is invigorating. It is an ideal time for planning, letter writing and realizing some of your more immediate objectives. Mental sharpness will govern throughout the end of the week.

28th Week/July 9–15

Friday the 9th calls for care in financial matters because lack of attention could put you in some difficulty. Step gingerly with people today; a subtle approach will be useful. You will find that much can be accomplished through the judicious application of pressure and encouragement to those people who work with you. The same kind of sensitivity will serve you at home.

Saturday the 10th is a good day to clear up residual money concerns or rectify business difficulties; these sorts of transactions could be particularly lucrative. Your mate or another loved one will be especially helpful, and it is a good time to discuss practical matters with family members. Others will generally be very cooperative and amenable to listening to your point of view. Your strength and vision will be appreciated.

Sunday the 11th will offer an opportunity to share familial warmth and also to complete a creative undertaking that has no practical end other than the enjoyment of doing it. The early afternoon hours will be most fruitfully spent in the bosom of kinsfolk, perhaps with a visit to an elderly relative. The mood will change after dinner, and you should capitalize on your quiet contentment by solitary work on a favorite hobby.

Monday the 12th it will be best to be as honest and aboveboard as possible with your associates at work. Secret arrangements are not favored today, and the support of people in the background will contribute to your success. Watch for indications of an argument early in the afternoon and avoid entanglement by immersing yourself in professional duties.

Tuesday the 13th finds you involved with influential people to hammer out agreements or contracts that have been in dispute for quite some time. Personal health may interfere with planned activities; be mindful of possible injury to the legs. Financial matters may cause an upset at home, and your partner will not cooperate with your plan for a whimsical purchase.

Wednesday the 14th will be marred by lingering frustration. Some thought may be helpful to illuminate ways to profit from past mistakes. You may be better off arranging to work alone since you are easily annoyed by the foibles of co-workers. Oddly enough, given your irritability, the evening is likely to be spent in a large crowd, perhaps at the theater or a sporting event.

Thursday the 15th will be a quiet day, and there will be few demands on your attention. It will be a good day for balancing the checkbook or doing other accounting tasks, but large-scale financial decisions should be postponed until a later date. You may be easily bored, but you can get a lot of small tedious jobs out of the way if you simply take them one at a time.

Weekly Summary

You would have to be a diplomat to preserve good relations considering the tension level early in the week. Attention will also have to be directed to financial issues since there will be an opportunity to make money through careful investing. Time should also be allocated to discuss practical matters with the family.

Some behind-the-scenes manipulations will be helpful to you at work early in the week, but in general clandestine moves are not favored and honesty is called for. The best course of action will be quiet, solitary concentration on a project you need to be working on. Midweek is an odd time that will see some resolution to outstanding issues at work. There may be a senseless dispute at home related to a purchase you want to make that your mate doesn't approve of.

The last few days of the week will be very favorable to individual efforts. You will be impatient with other people so time spent alone will be most productive. There may be an outing involving a group of people. As the week comes to an end, you will be able to dispose of many small, nagging responsibilities.

29th Week/July 16–22

Friday the 16th is a good day for communicating with distant people, and an effort to mend fences or rekindle dormant friendships can be rewarding. Personal health is on the upswing, and you will feel more physical energy than in recent days. Legal or financial affairs are the source of unexpected good news. The afternoon is appropriate for a self-improvement project.

Saturday the 17th be careful, you might eat or drink too much today. You may find your mental and physical needs are at odds. You want to play and while away the day, but responsibilities related to work prevent you from indulging your desires. Later your attention turns toward health considerations, and an exercise program or purchase of equipment occupies your thoughts.

Sunday the 18th you will feel passionate about things. Try not to become obsessive about work and attempt to make the most of the time available. Your partner might feel restless, so find out why or it might get very confusing. Control your passion and use the day to reflect on the situation; eventually things will begin to make more sense as open communication is restored.

Monday the 19th brings another burst of energy to your social life. Political issues will be raised, and you want to get involved or make a contribution. Aquarius will spend a great deal of time talking and arguing with friends, and although the passion might boil over a bit, there will be no lasting animosity. Give some space to your mate rather than trying to force him or her to be open when not appropriate. Avoid impulsive actions.

Tuesday the 20th will bring a pleasant sense of well-being, direction and purpose. You feel warm and friendly toward people and want to contribute something to the welfare of others. Coupled with your compassion is a sober and realistic view of life that makes you realize you can't change the world, although you know you can make a difference. Take a businesslike approach to your tasks.

Wednesday the 21st finds deadlines beginning to loom ominously, but inventive friends help you regain a proper perspective. Pay attention to your actions because you are slightly irritable and may overreact to slight setbacks and have a tendency to be accident-prone. Make plans by yourself, but be sure to discuss them with your mate or friend and perhaps parents.

Thursday the 22nd you will feel very affectionate toward loved ones, but there is also a tendency to be overprotective and smothering with your love. Think about yourself and your own needs. You will enjoy being surrounded by people who are connected to your past, perhaps old friends you haven't seen for a long time, but don't let nostalgia cause you to lose sight of the future. Beware of someone's ulterior motives.

Weekly Summary

The week begins on several positive notes. You feel healthy, are able to improve some strained relationships, and there is good news related to personal business considerations. Later you will want to be self-indulgent and cast your troubles to the winds but will be prevented from doing so by pressing responsibilities. Although you struggle, you probably won't get too much done. There is danger of becoming obsessive.

Passion will begin to well up in your breast, but it will be centered on the social problems that plague our society rather than on more personal concerns. Your mate might have to bear some of the brunt of your heady feelings. A realistic view does return, and with a level head you consider what you can do to address some of these societal issues. You feel warm and connected to something larger than yourself.

Work-related stress tends to build toward the end of the week. You may be on edge and clumsy as a result, but a friend will help you to regain control of your emotions. Because of nostalgia, you may be overly worried about your loved ones. You can avoid this and escape the past by concentrating on your own needs.

30th Week/July 23–29

Friday the 23rd brings intense emotions and a feeling of sensitivity but you are content with your life. Your somber attitude may dispose you toward strong, clear-thinking people for intellectually stimulating conversation. Your lack of superficiality will greatly enhance your romantic relationships. A new closeness will be established. Weekend travel promises a lot of fun.

Saturday the 24th might spark unnecessary conflicts. Don't look to others for reinforcement of what you know in your heart to be true. Do what you know is right regardless of the immediate impression it gives. Others will soon realize the honesty and integrity of your actions and will appreciate them. If you are not demanding, others will take you for granted.

Sunday the 25th is a great day for a relaxed outing with a small group. Warm feelings are plentiful, and there is an abiding sense of pleasure and bonhomie. Your sense of humor is at its sharpest and you keep the atmosphere light and joyous. There may be travel difficulties, perhaps an auto breakdown or flat tire, but you won't let it dampen the spirit of the day.

Monday the 26th you take the helm at work and lead your colleagues in a day of very fruitful discussions. Your personal magnetism will be irresistible. You are vigorous and brimming with confidence and optimism. Be careful not to let it go to your head, and beware of the lurking danger of self-inflation and conceitedness. Relationships are satisfying, but there is a potential for trouble due to your overpossessiveness.

Tuesday the 27th is a very stimulating day. There is an inclination to act independently and to move forward alone without recourse to others for assistance. It is appropriate to plan for the future and to realize some long-standing aspirations. New business ventures are favored. Friends will be helpful and offer advice that confirms your own conclusions.

Wednesday the 28th finds Aquarius with good rein on the emotions, making it a propitious time for self-analysis. Because deductive thought and communication are at their peaks, you should seize this opportunity to convey ideas and get points across to others. If you take the initiative now, you will reap the benefits for months to come. Personal interaction is vital today.

Thursday the 29th presents an excellent opportunity to make some changes in your personal life. It will be a day of acute intuition and heightened sensitivity to the inner needs of others. You should reevaluate relationships and make sure they are not just comfortable old habits that have outlived their usefulness. It's a good time to freshen things up. Your evening may be rife with amorous adventures.

Weekly Summary

Your emotions are very strong at the beginning of the week. Your serious mood will be tempered by a sensitivity that will draw you to strong people. Likewise, there will be much activity related to romantic relationships. Your empathetic nature may lead to some confusion and possible conflicts, but it is important that you have the courage of your convictions and remain true to your ideals.

Later in the weekend and early during the week, you will exhibit a high degree of personal magnetism. Others will look to you for guidance and advice. Your sense of humor will be a major lift to the spirits of the group you spend time with. Your independence enables you to see your own needs and best interests with clarity, making it a good time for formulating future plans and undertaking challenging new ventures.

Emotional stability and an ability to see yourself honestly and practically will continue through the end of the week. It's still a good time to assume leadership roles so others can benefit from your own good fortune. There is also plenty of energy for examining your life.

31st Week/July 30–August 5

Friday the 30th Aquarius is somewhat irritable. You may feel unsatisfied looking back at the week to review what was done and how much was left undone. There is a proclivity to be impulsive and want to escape from restrictions, but you have pressing obligations that must be met. Thoughts turn toward the home and building or remodeling. It might involve a struggle, but eventually you will be able to get hold of your emotions today.

Saturday the 31st is a very pleasant day. You return to the positive aura that has prevailed this month and are again able to relate well to people. It's a terrific day to cast your concerns to the wind and to enjoy the company of friends in a leisurely group activity. Also spend time doing yard work or some other relaxing task. You might take a short trip with family or friends.

Sunday August 1st your priorities may have to be altered, with work deemphasized and a greater focus placed on the home. Sometimes it takes a conscious effort to restore a healthy balance. Events may converge to present you with an opportunity for an intense emotional experience. An old relationship might undergo tension, but the strain shouldn't be irreparable.

Monday the 2nd is a good day for Aquarius to get a lot of work completed, either alone or with others. Satisfaction is most likely to come from a pivotal role where your leadership and charisma will be greatly valued. The tempo of social interchange is increasing and you may spend a fair amount of time talking to friends. Exposure to new ideas is from an unlikely source.

Tuesday the 3rd the tide turns, and this is not a productive day in the literal sense. You feel dreamy and otherworldly, and your thoughts tend to wander. You should heed these flights of fancy to understand where they might be leading. Relationships are unpredictable right now, so give them some thought, but delay any important decisions until tomorrow.

Wednesday the 4th you may have houseguests. Relatives may contribute time or advice to help you overcome inertia and sloth. You feel introverted but are willing to listen to suggestions from outside your immediate sphere of contacts. Business takes a turn for the better, and you make a major breakthrough on a project you work on. Someone admires you from afar.

Thursday the 5th Aquarius clarifies plans about the house that have been slowly taking shape these past few weeks. Now is the time to move forward. Share your energy with your mate or a close friend. Channels of communication are wide open. Discuss what has been on your mind, and it will become clearer to both of you. The financial situation is in flux, but it's a good time to make joint decisions.

Weekly Summary

As the week begins your high spirits diminish as you look back on the previous week. You may feel a pang of guilt about not making the most of the opportunities you had. You may desire to evade your duties, but you know that will only make you feel worse. Later you get a hold of yourself and enter the weekend feeling much more contented and satisfied. You should spend time with friends and relax into the comfortable sharing and pleasant warmth of the group.

You may come to the realization that you have been devoting too much attention to your job and not enough to your family. A shift of focus will allow a greater range of emotional satisfaction and won't necessarily mean that you neglect your work responsibilities. You have enough vitality for both. You will get immediate confirmation of this through the abundant energy and enthusiasm you feel at the workplace and your contribution in a leadership position.

A wistful state will engulf you later in the week that will make it advisable to postpone crucial decisions. You will be better served by paying attention to your dreams and noticing their direction. The result will be an immediate return of good fortune.

32nd Week/August 6–12

Friday the 6th you should plan to work on projects related to the home. There are things in the attic that will evoke fond memories and cause you to return to a hobby long abandoned. Since music will play a role in the day, perhaps you will find an instrument you haven't played in years. You will derive inordinate pleasure from tinkering or casual play. A telephone call may bring surprising news about your job.

Saturday the 7th sees daily life thrown out of kilter by an illness in the family. There may be a visit to the

192 / DAILY FORECAST—AQUARIUS

hospital at midday. Financial concerns will be the topic of conversation among family members, and disputes will occur before an amicable solution is reached. Emotions will be raw most of the day, and you will be very excitable and impatient. Listen with an open mind.

Sunday the 8th is a good day to hide out and focus on a project involving writing or making something. You can lose yourself in the work you are doing with your hands and begin to regain control of your emotions and forget the upsets of yesterday. You may communicate with someone from overseas and spend time making plans for a trip later in the year.

Monday the 9th finds Aquarius with a very realistic view of life that enables you to persevere in spite of any strain or adversity. Tender emotions are brought to the fore, and there will be a vibrant closeness with your mate or closest friend. Your exceptional patience demonstrates your strength of character. Seemingly unsurmountable problems may emerge, but they can be solved without much difficulty.

Tuesday the 10th calls for caution because you lean toward volatility and brash behavior today. Perhaps some fine-tuning may be called for in your immediate personal life. These alternations should not be major ones but must be constructive. Pay attention to finances since minor difficulties may be brewing that will surface in the near future. Be loyal to a family member.

Wednesday the 11th is a favorable day for advancement in business. There might be a dinner in an elegant restaurant with an associate that will have a beneficial effect on your future. Agreements made with friends will come into play in a positive manner in business or at home. Influential people may lend support in a subtle way to express appreciation for your reliability.

Thursday the 12th is a quiet day that offers the chance to relax and enjoy the fruits of earlier labors. You might be presented with a scheme to make some quick money, but be careful and don't make hasty decisions. Romance may insinuate itself into business matters, but this presents the danger of misunderstanding and its resultant stress. The loyalty of Aquarius is tested.

Weekly Summary

The week begins with an amusing sense of carefree fun, but it will be short-circuited by health problems the following day. There may be a family dispute concerning finances, and the result of the day's tension will be an inescapable state of agitation. It is best to end the weekend by losing yourself in a hobby or other activity that will take your mind off problems and restore some emotional stability.

Patience and tenderness mark the middle of the week when the upsets of the weekend are finally left behind. You can face challenges with the clear head and a presence of mind that had been missing. It will be needed to help you avert financial difficulties you might otherwise have to confront in the near future.

Business prospects take a very favorable turn later in the week. You may get behind-the-scenes help that shows the esteem in which you are held by some important people. Agreements made earlier will become a factor in the good fortune you will experience. Don't be hasty later in the week; be skeptical of any investment opportunities you may be offered. Things seem better at first glance than they truly are. There will be exciting romantic developments at the end of the week.

194 / DAILY FORECAST—AQUARIUS

33rd Week/August 13–19

Friday the 13th is a day Aquarius need not fear. Good fortune abounds and nearly everything attempted will work out beautifully. Your energy is so strong that friends and family will all share your good feeling and be sympathetic to your every desire. It's a good day to select gifts because you're so in tune with the needs of others. An act of kindness will be much appreciated.

Saturday the 14th is extremely auspicious for socializing. Aquarius feels gregarious and derives great enjoyment from being with people. It's a good time to entertain at home or to do some work toward making the home more attractive or livable. You tend to indulge yourself, so an expensive dinner might be in order. Glamorous surroundings might set the stage for an amorous interlude.

Sunday the 15th brings a distracted, distant state of mind. Spend time with a loved one or with a group that is compatible with your interests. Just staying at home is also appropriate. Domestic surroundings appeal to you more than usual for the next several days. See close relatives and put any smoldering conflicts to rest once and for all. Take advantage of the placid harmony.

Monday the 16th is filled with vigor that promotes meaningful communication. Use this period to align yourself with co-workers and superiors so that everyone's efforts are maximized to meet current objectives. There is a stress on independence and personal freedom, but don't ignore the ties that bind you to those who are most important to you. Health is optimal.

Tuesday the 17th may bring an internecine power struggle to upset your general upbeat mood. Close family members might take to game playing, perhaps leading to a significant change in domestic life. Business travel is likely. You may meet a fascinating new person and there will be a mutual romantic interest. Take a moment to reflect if you are living up to your ideals.

Wednesday the 18th Aquarius feels recharged in both mind and body. Throughout the course of the day you see the world as your playground, a place where you can accomplish anything you set your mind to. Set your sights high because no matter what you attempt, you will not miss the mark. Take fullest advantage because days like this don't come often enough.

Thursday the 19th sees Aquarius' relationships working even more smoothly than usual. The dichotomy between ego and id that sometimes creates confusion is receding now. All aspects of the self are working together smoothly, making this another productive day. You are very sensitive to those around you so group efforts are highly recommended.

Weekly Summary

You begin the week by defying the common superstition and enjoying good fortune on Friday the 13th. Do whatever you think best because it will work out for you. You follow that with a day of socializing that will be very satisfying. The rest of the weekend is spent enjoying the comforts of home and family. You will float dreamily on the peaceful feelings around you.

You will bound into the workweek energized, independent and compassionate. This energy should be utilized to work on lingering problems disrupting the family because you will be an exceptional mediator of any conflict. This ability will also be helpful later in the week because there may be a conflict at home that you will no longer be able to respond to as creatively or effectively as you had earlier. There may be some changes that will cause you to go through a period of intense self-criticism.

Another reversal will occur at the end of the week and spirits will once again soar. You will get a lot done while you ride the crest of this sudden wave. Again, you will be highly instrumental to those around you who bask in the light of your vitality and optimism. Good relations will be abundant.

34th Week/August 20–26

Friday the 20th finds Aquarius sensitive to both his own feelings and those of others. Communication will be efficient because there is an enhanced ability to listen and comprehend what is said. Casual acquaintances will count on you and ask you to help them solve their problems. You radiate warmth and good cheer and have an uplifting effect on the people around you.

Saturday the 21st you should make an effort to avoid negative people because they will undermine your ebullient state of mind. It is a good day to spend with those close friends who you know won't try to poison your mood. There is a strong craving for excitement and a pleasant feeling of restlessness. Your high energy may be resented by your mate who is perhaps feeling a little under the weather. Be sure to try to buck them up.

Sunday the 22nd may bring a chance encounter with an exciting new person. If that doesn't happen, the probability is good for a surprise encounter with an old friend who has not been seen or heard from recently. Carefully investigate new propositions that will be presented to you. Keep an open mind because some of these may be lucrative if you are willing to take risks.

Monday the 23rd presents an opportunity to make positive changes. Domestic life will bring rich emotional rewards. Understanding will deepen because both your intuition and logic are acute. Existing relationships will bring more satisfaction than they have before. There may be new discoveries about the self that shed fresh light on past difficulties.

Tuesday the 24th is a useful day for attending to neglected tasks you need to be free of. Activities should be confined to routine affairs as it is not a good time to try something new or adventurous. Don't sit back and do nothing, but lay the groundwork for future plans. There may be a last-minute change of plans, but don't let it upset you as it might be for the best.

Wednesday the 25th will be marred by a lack of discipline, and it will be next to impossible to get anything done. It's a good day to keep to yourself, relax, catch up with your reading and avoid disrupting relationships with your negative energy. If you are able to find an inner focus, you should look to the future and try to envision the course of action that will best meet your goals and suit your needs.

Thursday the 26th Aquarius is very demanding of other people but somewhat unwilling to offer anything in return. You are undecided whether you want to be alone or with other people. A woman friend will help you get out of the funk you're in if you heed her wise words. Don't drink too much and be careful of spending more than you had planned.

Weekly Summary

Sensitivity enables Aquarius to continue to be a positive influence on others early in the week. There will be a willingness to listen and understand that will help others find their way out of troubles. You will be a source of light. Later, there will be a danger of others draining you of your positive energy, so conserve it by hoarding it more carefully and sharing it with the one person who most needs it at this time.

Restlessness and a need for excitement will be prevalent later in the weekend, and early in the workweek you will realize that these things can be easily found at home. You now can see certain parts of your life from a different perspective. Routine matters will command some attention, but that is for the best because it is not a good time for adventurous new undertakings.

Later in the week there will be a loss of focus and a frustrating inability to accomplish much. It will be better to keep to yourself rather than risk damage to relationships with unwanted interference. The mood will be unsettled and you may be confused. Do you want to be social or do you want to be alone? You may overindulge but a friend will get you back on track.

35th Week/August 27–September 2

Friday the 27th finds colleagues very cooperative and willing to make an extra effort to help you get an assignment completed on time. On the other hand, your mate will be obstinate, and the situation at home is more stressful than at work. A complete turnabout occurs later in the evening allowing bonds to be reinforced. Disappointments and frustrations will vanish.

Saturday the 28th Aquarius might be troubled by a difference of opinion that causes an upset and derails an initial good mood. You will be accident-prone, so try to abandon your anger lest it lead to broken dishes at home. Don't let uncertainty about the course of your relationship tempt you to spoil what can be a meaningful afternoon and evening together.

Sunday the 29th you will spend a fair amount of time making long-distance telephone calls. You might be put in a bind by a request for a loan from a close friend to whom you owe a favor. Financial matters are a common topic of the day, and you may be annoyed because you have other things on your mind. To divert yourself, plan a gathering for later in the week.

Monday the 30th inclines Aquarius to be secretive and to keep ideas and feelings to himself. This state will make you want to avoid people, but there will be a frantic pace at work that will preclude this. You are not easily influenced by others but will reluctantly do your part to avert a crisis in the workplace. The confusion will be pervasive and will follow you home as well.

Tuesday the 31st sees romantic or sexual relations considerably enriched because communications have moved past the superficial level. You will spend much time in serious conversation with your partner. You now get that quiet, solitary day at work you had planned for yesterday. You will be gratified that your affairs are in much better order than you had suspected. You will feel happy and content.

Wednesday September 1st gives a pleasing sensation of restiveness. You probably want to shake the foundations of the world to startle it out of what you see as complacency and self-satisfaction. You should seek out stimulating people and will probably go to a place you had never considered before. You will not accept old routines or commonplace situations.

Thursday the 2nd will be favorable for group efforts. Relations will be harmonious, particularly with the opposite sex, and there may be an opportunity to kindle a new romance. You are perceptive to other people's needs and willing to give of yourself. You feel very self-confident and energized and resolve to eliminate tiresome habits and routines from your daily life.

Weekly Summary

There is stress at home early in the week that will be countered by willing assistance proffered by associates on the job. Things improve but you will carry a bad mood into the next day that will cause further strain. Try to forget it and enjoy the good feelings that remain a fundamental reality beneath the confusion. Financial matters may also seem troubling, but you will come to realize that there is no problem.

You may want to avoid other people, but because of demands at work will be unable to do so. You do what needs to be done but find it very draining. The next day will allow you the opportunity to have the peaceful day you had sought. You are more concerned with romance than business and much progress is made in this regard.

By the end of the week, you will be ready to make some noise and will want to give the world a wake-up call because you feel strongly that it's needed. You feel good about yourself but frustrated by the complacency around you. This mood calms down a bit, but you will continue feeling the need to promote change and to avoid the tyranny of old habits and routines.

36th Week/September 3–9

Friday the 3rd you will be buoyant and impatient for the weekend to begin. Romantic energy is in the air, buzzing like a late-summer bee, and you are eager to make the most of it. It's a good time for small favors or gifts to let people know they are appreciated. If you follow the call to adventure wherever it may lead, there will be no cause for regrets.

Saturday the 4th you may be torn between nostalgia for the fading summer and eagerness to embrace the approaching autumn. Try not to indulge your tendency to be hard on yourself; don't waste energy regretting missed opportunities, but rather resolve to make the most of things in the future. Don't sit at home lost in thought or making plans; be impulsive and go out to do something unusual.

Sunday the 5th will involve travel of some sort, either going to meet friends or having them travel to be with you. Intense social energies are afoot today, and you cannot get into a casual holiday mood. There are indications of an impending breakup of a long-standing relationship that will be a shock to everyone involved. You feel a new appreciation for your mate.

Monday the 6th you will be bothered by a sense that something has been forgotten, and this will distract you from simply enjoying the day. Do your best to forget this notion since good fortune is indicated in business. There will be warm relations between you and family members. Indulge yourself; be carefree and peaceful on a day when loved ones are on your wavelength.

Tuesday the 7th is a good day for creative and speculative ventures. Much will be accomplished, and you can approach the rest of the year with a sense that you are the master of your own destiny with all aspects of your life fully under control. You will have a hard time getting machinery or electronic equipment to cooperate as you may be a bit clumsy.

Wednesday the 8th finds work interrupted by the health problem of a co-worker, and you wind up spending most of the afternoon trying to make up for lost time. Good productivity in business projects is indicated, but be careful not to misplace something you will need to do the job. Home will be harmonious and tender feelings will abound during the early part of the evening.

Thursday the 9th preoccupies Aquarius with thoughts of the home, wondering how a basically satisfying environment can be made even more pleasing. It might be time for renovating or redesigning part of the house. Finances are favorable, but there may be a heated discussion of your plans. Your timing is right, so stick to your guns but in a cordial manner that won't offend.

Weekly Summary

The week opens with high spirits and anticipation of the weekend because you feel the irresistible pull of romantic energy. The call to adventure will be very strong and the time is right to follow it. You experience something of a turnaround and will find your thoughts suddenly looking backward rather than forward; fight this impulse and make something exciting happen. You may be pensive during holiday gatherings and get involved in rather deep discussions. The force of the past continues to exert its influence into the middle of the week, and you should continue to do your best to resist it.

As you return to work, you finally see what has been troubling you and can easily resolve the problem. You will finally be able to look forward to the rest of the year, and the only problem you encounter is due to your own awkwardness.

Someone else's health will cause a disruption toward the end of the week, but nonetheless you will be highly productive. The week will come to an end with your attention directed toward making improvements in your home. You may find ways to spruce up both the physical and the emotional environment that will make it more conducive to harmonious living.

37th Week/September 10–16

Friday the 10th there will be a surfeit of sentiment in the workplace, perhaps a party for a departing co-worker of whom you are very fond. There may be a breakthrough related to ongoing business that will make you look very good in the eyes of your superiors. Your pride will be bolstered by a demonstration of appreciation from your friends, so do your best to ignore any jealousy or resentment.

Saturday the 11th Aquarius finds his or her partner to be demanding and somewhat obstreperous. It may seem that everything you try to do doesn't work, so roll with the punches as much as possible. Don't waste time worrying about the relationship; your moods just happen to be out of sync today. Put off shared activities until tomorrow and seek the fellowship of friends who better match your state of mind.

Sunday the 12th is a day to spend with your partner to savor the particularly harmonious relations between you. If you are single, spend time in an environment where you have the opportunity to meet others because good fortune related to romance is indicated. Your level of clarity is elevated today, and you have heightened intellectual and creative abilities.

Monday the 13th demonstrates the affection between members of the immediate family. This gives you a profound appreciation for the joys of domesticity. Final touches will be completed that have held up the satisfactory outcome of a joint venture. You will be given a challenging assignment that will demonstrate that someone important has a lot of faith in you.

Tuesday the 14th brings events that dredge up repressed resentments, and this might cause you to lose sight of important work issues. There will be obstacles throughout the day, but close family relationships will exert a stabilizing influence that will help you ride out the storm. Concentrate on the bigger picture rather than dwelling on the minor upsets of the day.

Wednesday the 15th ushers in a period that does not favor interaction with others so refrain from group activities if possible. It is a good time to look ahead toward obligations that will have to be met during the week ahead. Children will help you restore a happy emotional balance. There might be a visit from distant relatives who will come bearing good news.

Thursday the 16th Aquarius tends to be touchy and somewhat distraught. Despite this, it's a beneficial day in terms of relationships at work. You will probably lend a helping hand, but be careful not to get frustrated at the response it elicits. You may be giving off incongruous signals. Houseguests can cause some consternation but they contribute warmth and happiness.

Weekly Summary

Mixed emotions will prevail at the workplace early in the week, with both sadness and happiness in attendance. Personally, things will be quite positive with some significant career development occurring. Early in the weekend there may be stress at home, but it's only the result of a temporary mood mismatch. Nothing more serious is indicated; spend time with friends instead. The rest of the weekend will see a strong closeness, and romantic responses will be strong.

Mental acuity and good fortune will be the rule toward midweek but it will be short-lived. The home will be important and will stabilize what has in other respects become an unsettled week. There will be another example of the esteem in which you are held at work. At this point in time it will be better to use it as a springboard to help you look toward the future rather than getting lost in the problems of the present.

At the end of the week there is some difficulty communicating, and that will be frustrating. Children will help you restore the proper emotional balance to your life. You will be excitable and tend to overreact.

38th Week/September 17–23

Friday the 17th will be a reckless period for you. Be careful not to leap to the wrong conclusion, especially about matters related to business. It is best to avoid making any decisive moves now. It is, however, a good time for amorous activities and bonds can be strengthened. The winds of change are blowing your way, and you will find romance in an entirely new direction.

Saturday the 18th finds Aquarius seeking stimulation through new people and participation in community service activities. There is a high likelihood of an agreement by the extended family concerning an elderly member. Animals will play a part in the day, perhaps in the form of a trip to the zoo or a visit to the vet.

Sunday the 19th features love relationships and the sublime harmony they foster. To expand on this felicity, Aquarius recruits other people to join the day's activities. You should go to great lengths to gather a simpatico group of friends to spend the day together. Relaxed conversation and sharing predominate. When everyone goes home, the residual glow will suffuse the evening with joy and extend itself into the week.

Monday the 20th causes Aquarius to set the pace for harmony and good vibrations among those people lucky enough to be near him or her. Everyone will want to partake of the radiant aura that emanates from your inner self. You will find yourself attracting someone decidedly out of the ordinary who may offer romantic possibilities. If you already have a mate, there will be a new burst of electricity between you.

Tuesday the 21st sees a considerable amount of time frittered away in daydreaming about the future. Despite your best intentions, little will be accomplished. It is recommended that you set your sights on easily attainable goals to avoid frustration. Since you are impelled to wander down the paths of the imagination, devote your energies to a creative, aesthetic project.

Wednesday the 22nd Aquarius may be under scrutiny, perhaps having an evaluation at work. A favorable outcome is indicated although there will be a period of uncertainty. Now is the time to play your hunches as intuitive capabilities are soaring. The evening is appropriate for contemplating spiritual or philosophic questions. Follow thoughts where they lead.

Thursday the 23rd can have many different aspects due to an unsettled and troubling emotional issue. You might find yourself unable to resist compulsive behavior or giving in to sudden unwholesome urges. The constructive side of this condition is that it prompts you to lend a helping hand to those in need. Watch your feelings and you can control your fate today.

Weekly Summary

Impulsiveness will be strong early in the week, making it a bad time for weighty decisions. Romantic life will be very active. The overall tendency, however, is toward change. Group activity will be frequent and time will be spent negotiating family business. Intense social energy instills Aquarius with a contended enthusiasm and a warm glow that will last well into the week.

The week is one when good relations and strong interpersonal communication will be the rule. This positive energy helps attract someone who offers some exciting romantic possibilities. You will be able to get a lot done with a seemingly limitless source of energy.

Imagination and creative energy change the focus of your attention later in the week, and instead of being group oriented and pragmatic, you will devote yourself to working on an artistic project simply for the sheer fun of it. Later in the week there is some pressure at work, but you can meet the challenge with the mastery that is yours at this point in time. The week ends with a bit of befuddlement as you will be caught up in a changing mood and won't be sure of your direction.

39th Week/September 24–30

Friday the 24th Aquarius will feel invigorated, enthusiastic and fully in control of his life. Change is in the air at home, but it must be managed with style and grace to lead in a positive direction. It is a day of relaxed banter rather than serious conversation with your mate or a close friend, but within this context some serious new ideas will be developing. Spend time with children.

Saturday the 25th will be less relaxed as attention is drawn toward serious concerns and future plans. It may be time to start considering a job change, not due to unhappiness but because of persistent questions about the path your career has been taking. A move to a different part of the country might be discussed with your partner or friends. Because of a relationship with a young person, this might not be for the best.

Sunday the 26th will be a more laid back day. Although you want to devote time to serious considerations, the mood around you is relaxed and jovial. Rather than resist it, put your questions aside, kick back and enjoy life. An extended meal will take up most of the early evening. It's a good time to ask questions and get different reactions to them.

Monday the 27th Aquarius' restlessness will be countered by a satisfying sense of accomplishment and pride. You will look back at what you have achieved and realize your intrinsic value to those who share your life. Communication is optimal and you feel a strong sense of place and purpose. Suddenly you get a more cogent perspective on those questions on your mind.

Tuesday the 28th you may have a strong desire to set the world on fire, at least that part of it you inhabit. You are efficient and focused and will be a whirlwind of energy, feeling like you can get three days' work done today. Tackle the most unappealing tasks first to get them out of the way. Be sure to share your energy with people in your life rather than overwhelming them.

Wednesday the 29th there will be a reversal and you may end up feeling exhausted. Take quiet stock of where you are and where you need to be going. The company of children will be soothing and help you preserve some of your vitality. Relationships should be very stable and comfortable. Home is where the heart is and you know exactly where that is.

Thursday the 30th Aquarius should make an effort to steer clear of downbeat people who do their best to sow seeds of discontent. Get the most out the state you're in without letting anyone undermine it. Take charge of your life through the strength of character that gives you a subtle but pronounced advantage over those who oppose you. Home, family, and career are in a happy balance.

Weekly Summary

Your mood will stabilize again early in the week and Aquarius will be very relaxed and able to meet the challenges in his path. These involve an examination of the direction life is taking and a reevaluation of goals. This will engender a more sober mood, and some tension may develop as complex issues are addressed, but this will be short-lived and won't be overly oppressive.

Your ability to help others will aid you early in the workweek as you utilize your ability to give good advice and find the wisdom to look at your own concerns with objectivity and clarity. From this recognition you will glean the energy to tackle problems and responsibilities with enthusiasm, intelligence and ambition. This ability will also function to draw your mate closer.

Relationships will be the most important aspect of your life by the end of the week. You depend on the warmth and support they provide and will have a deeper appreciation of their value as your energy wanes with the week. Be careful not to let a negative person undermine the good feelings finally taking root after some struggle. Children will figure prominently all week.

40th Week/October 1–7

Friday October 1st might bring an emotional conflict with someone important in your life. Try not to get too upset as no major problem will result, but it will tend to undercut your good mood. Keep your nose to the grindstone as you have a lot to do. Financial matters may be a topic over lunch; don't be overly cautious because an interesting opportunity will be presented.

210 / DAILY FORECAST—AQUARIUS

Saturday the 2nd will probably be a day of travel. Relaxation and exciting good times are indicated. Romantic energies are running high, so enjoy the partner you have or cultivate a new one, preferably an Aries. Love may be waiting where you least expect it. You will spend some money, but the result is a much-needed new outlook. Shopping expeditions lead to bargains.

Sunday the 3rd will be another day of continuing change. A new person in your life will make tried-and-true answers seem dull and boring. Don't fight your feelings, you have good judgment, and your emotions are in sync with your intellect and won't lead you too far astray. It's a good day to slack off a bit and stop censoring yourself.

Monday the 4th brings pleasant interactions between you and most people you encounter. You are invigorated by recent developments and emanate positive energy. Someone you know is in need but won't ask for help. Make an effort to find this person and do what you can to lift his or her spirits. It is definitely a day not to hide your light; what you give will return twofold.

Tuesday the 5th finds Aquarius in an unpredictable state, ready to swing between exuberance and melancholy at the slightest provocation. The excitement and disarray you see doesn't really concern you, but you have trouble avoiding entanglement due to your curiosity and willingness to lend a helping hand. Pay attention to your own interests to minimize any disturbance.

Wednesday the 6th might see your spirits sagging a bit. Your plans have not quite reached the point you had hoped, and you are disappointed that you have let yourself be distracted. It's a good time to strengthen your resolve and try harder the second time. You want to save the world but have to remember that the contribution you make, however small, does help.

Thursday the 7th you may feel the weight of the world on your shoulders, but you must remember that you have the power to cast it off. If you look in the right direction, the answer is obvious. Remind yourself that even the longest journey begins with the first step, no matter how tenuous or timid. Take time to examine exactly where you are, where you want to be and the direction in which you are heading.

Weekly Summary

Don't let your mood be undermined by interpersonal difficulties that trouble you early in the week. It will be to your advantage to take this opportunity to get much accomplished. You should also be open to some exciting new possibilities that may crop up. The prescription for the first few days of the week is to relax and go with the flow. You will be surprised at where it might lead.

Your generosity will be called on later in the week. You feel close to people and will be asked to make an effort on someone else's behalf. It will be worth your while to do so. Things will get somewhat chaotic, and despite your best efforts you will be involved. It is better not to avoid this but to follow your normal urge to lend a hand where you can. Be sure you don't lose sight of your own private concerns.

At the end of the week, you will feel a little let down and burdened by the troubles of the world. Remember to concentrate on your considerable abilities and talents and stop worrying about those things that you can't possibly change. Your efforts are important and do make a difference.

41st Week/October 8–14

Friday the 8th is a day that Aquarius should find to be extremely satisfying. You are concerned with making life more rewarding and events today will point you in precisely the direction you need to travel. Heightened communication between you and your mate fosters exceptional harmony at home. Let someone know they have been helpful and that you appreciate it.

Saturday the 9th involves you in serious talks that bring you closer to your mate. Health worries that have clouded both your minds will no longer be a factor and the atmosphere between you is considerably brightened. You will work on a joint project and then enjoy a relaxed and tranquil time. You might find yourself feeling self-indulgent about food but you deserve to be.

Sunday the 10th you will participate in a group or gathering with an altruistic goal. You might be inclined to duck your usual leadership role, but because the group depends on you, you will do what is necessary for its sake. Remember not to drain yourself by giving all your energy away; save some for yourself and the people at home. Emotional generosity is rewarding.

Monday the 11th gives you time to do some penetrating soul-searching to make sure your ideals and your actions are consistent. Pay attention to recent dreams. It's a time for giving to those people closest to you. Communication is good and you are willing to listen and share. You may have neglected someone, and this is your chance to make amends. A gift of yourself is always better than anything else.

Tuesday the 12th Aquarius feels lethargic and out of sorts as if in reaction to the generosity and high energy of recent days. This is likely to be a question of health rather than overwrought emotion. Slow down, listen to your body and give it what it needs. Remember the exercises you have resolved to do, and when you're tired, get some rest. Relocation of the workplace may bring both excitement and annoyance.

Wednesday the 13th brings exciting good news. Investments will be fruitful, and the financial worries that have intermittently plagued you will move closer to a successful dénouement. It is probably a good time to treat yourself well and make that major purchase you have been considering. A friend might volunteer some assistance, but beware of an ulterior motive behind the sudden generosity.

Thursday the 14th will be a day when emotions are more intense than in recent weeks. Aquarius will be passionate about things that just yesterday were taken with a grain of salt. This condition is related to an inner turmoil that has crept into your consciousness to become a factor in daily life. Examine your goals and try to live in accordance with your deep and ardent dreams. Be true to yourself.

Weekly Summary

This week starts off on a very straightforward path. You feel good about your life, have no confusion about what you need to be doing and can communicate exceptionally well with others. This will help you realize the strength of the bonds that connect you with someone else. You will find the time you share to be extremely rewarding. This vitality will continue through midweek, and you will be an important presence in groups.

Fatigue will creep into your life, and you feel worn out as the week winds down. You must tap into energy resources to allow yourself to continue to enjoy the good relations that have recently been the rule. There will be some good news about money matters that allows you to acquire a high-ticket item.

The week ends on a discordant note of emotional incoherence. Things that were not noteworthy early in the week will suddenly seem very troublesome, and you will be unable to reestablish the equanimity that had served you so well. This restlessness has its roots in some underlying uncertainty you have been neglecting. Self-examination will help you restore balance.

42nd Week/October 15–21

Friday the 15th Aquarius unites favorable circumstances with the requisite resources and accomplishes wonders. Good fortune will follow you throughout the day but will come to a disconcerting end by the middle of the evening with a minor accident in the home caused by clumsiness. Don't let this setback ruin what is essentially a good day. Efficient communication and a leadership role are emphasized.

Saturday the 16th is a good time to concentrate on solitary endeavors even if your plans were to relax and do nothing. Your precision and concentration will lead to high productivity so your time is well spent. The afternoon is better suited to casting worldly concerns to the wind and savoring the company of those people you most care about. The day is quiet but ultimately satisfying.

Sunday the 17th will be a day for intimate relationships, but remember that a positive attitude should always predominate. Be wary of attempts to manipulate your feelings and outbreaks of unprovoked jealousy. Your patience may be tried, but staying calm and collected will stand you in good stead. Don't try to complicate the issues, but rather speak clearly and directly.

Monday the 18th favors acting as the leader of a group, preferably in the evening hours. Volunteer work is indicated, perhaps related to a political or social organization. The workday will involve many interruptions and annoyances, but productivity will still be high. The demands of home and work will be well balanced. An open mind can short-circuit simmering conflicts.

Tuesday the 19th is a good day to commence any kind of investigation or study. You feel curious and have an extraordinary ability to assimilate new information and put it to effective use. You may solve a problem that has vexed the workplace for some time. Good spirits will follow you home, and romantic interest will be at a peak this evening. A commitment is in the making.

Wednesday the 20th will be very interesting. The tempo of activity will accelerate to a state of frantic confusion, but you will ride the wave like a champion surfer. Your presence of mind is exceptional, particularly in the morning hours. The evening will be one of calm contemplation, so there will be harmony at home.

Thursday the 21st will be another day of effervescent moods. You will be attuned to your surroundings and empathetic to people, but at the same time you want to avoid the real world and disappear into your own thoughts and dreams. Because of your otherworldliness, you may frustrate those who try to penetrate the haze in which you find yourself immersed.

Weekly Summary

Good fortune rules at the beginning of the week. You will be productive and establish a good rapport with the people around you. Don't let a minor misunderstanding at home ruin the day. Take time to relax and concentrate on hobbies and other individual projects.

Your mental clarity will enable you to garner much satisfaction from a quiet day.

Relationships may get a little rocky, but if you have the courage to face the music and be completely honest, you can steer clear of most of the difficulties that are threatening to spoil your mood. Your social energies will be productively directed toward a service group working on a social or political issue. Relations in the office will also be harmonious.

The end of the week finds you functioning at a high level of intellectual acuity that will make you a master problem-solver. This energy will also spark your romance and give it a lift. Your mood will grow increasingly unsettled throughout the week, and by its end you may be vacillating between opposite ends of the spectrum, pulled toward solitary pursuits and interests.

43rd Week/October 22–28

Friday the 22nd Aquarius will be concerned with enriching his or her life by finding ways to make it more profound and interesting. It is a time of extremely positive, creative evolution. Take the initiative and do those things you have dreamed about. Use your intuition; think things through slowly and carefully. This is a golden opportunity to cross a new threshold.

Saturday the 23rd sends a cresting wave of physical and mental energy surging through your body. You feel like you can do it all today, and this is close to the truth. Set no limits but reach for the sky, and you will amaze yourself and those around you with your mastery, ability and ambition. The only down side is a propensity for the grandiose and a lack of patience with those who aren't similarly blessed, so watch yourself.

Sunday the 24th Aquarius should guard against a crash after coming down from yesterday's incredible peak.

Today will still be a good day, but in comparison it just won't measure up. Still, don't lose sight of the benefits today does offer such as good communication and warm relations with your partner. Look for the subtle satisfactions that lurk in the heart of this placid day.

Monday the 25th is a good time for Aquarius to consider finances and make some far-reaching commitments. Force yourself to sidestep the Monday blahs and get some crucial work done that will affect the future. Look to an older person to offer some sound and useful advice and be ready to do the same for a younger acquaintance who looks up to you.

Tuesday the 26th you will want to hibernate and eschew all social contact. Small troubles may seem immense at the moment, but if you can wrestle off the prevailing mood, you will be able to view them realistically. You have a penchant for feeling sorry for yourself even though things are essentially working in your favor. Do not drink or take pills to elevate your mood.

Wednesday the 27th will be an enigmatic day. There is a strong contrast between negative and positive forces with one prevailing at work and the other at home. This dichotomy will frustrate you and make you feel physically ill. As always, try to remain calm and centered. Be satisfied doing as much as you can and don't overextend yourself. Also, do not exaggerate your difficulties.

Thursday the 28th will see harmony restored but it will be by the loss of positive energy and the temporary ascendancy of the negative. Events will seem to conspire against you on all fronts. There will be travel delays, spills and other annoyances. Late afternoon brings a turnaround precipitated by good news received from home. The health of a loved one improves.

Weekly Summary

The week begins with you reaching a new peak of energy and creativity that allows you to make outstanding headway toward realizing your objectives. It will be the kind of boost you often dream of, but this time it's real. Set your aim as high as you want because you can accomplish almost anything you set out to do. You won't waste this time but will make the absolute most of it and be proud of what you achieve.

Later in the weekend, you come down from this fabulous high, and although you still feel supreme mastery and control, there will be a lessening of your good fortune that might convince you that it's gone. Don't worry, it isn't. As you move into the workweek, the energy will continue to diminish, and you will begin to feel tired and lose sight of important realities. There is a danger of wallowing in self-pity that you must avoid.

Your ephemeral mood will continue its slow descent. Your spirits sag, and you feel that everything is conspiring against you. You begin to rebound, and as the week ends, you will be getting back on the upswing.

44th Week/October 29–November 4

Friday the 29th you will be revitalized and there will be a restoration of harmony in personal life. You will be able to accomplish much, both in terms of work and frivolous pursuits. Friends gravitate toward you and will want to share ideas. Be careful not to leave something important undone that may come back to haunt you. Romantic possibilities are very promising.

Saturday the 30th sees your attention drawn to the home and directed fix-up projects and renovations. Difficulty expressing ideas will create some friction. You know exactly what needs to be done but have a hard time convincing your partner to see it your way. A shopping expedition will help show you both the way to compromise. In the evening you may attend a banquet.

Sunday the 31st will be a peaceful, carefree day spent with family members. It is a good time to get a jump on holiday shopping and for buying a trinket for someone special. There may be a problem involving water, perhaps a leak or a clogged drain. Energy will flag later on, leading to the cancellation of a planned get-together and the avoidance of a looming conflict.

Monday November 1st Aquarius starts the week with a clear mind and a readiness to roll up his sleeves and get down to work. Your leadership abilities enable you to set the pace for your associates throughout the day. Don't overlook minute details that are important, and don't forget that this is a special day for someone in your life. A loving gesture will be long remembered.

Tuesday the 2nd finds health matters again demanding some attention. They will not, however, prevent this from being a day that is pivotal for your romantic future. Follow your heart and try not to censor your feelings. There is something cooking, and you need to halt your hectic pace to take the time to get a whiff of what's on the menu. The evening favors organizational activities centering around humanitarian causes.

Wednesday the 3rd will be very taxing both on the job and at home. Tension is escalating because you will feel overburdened and unable to get everything done on time. You are also distracted by romantic misadventures. Someone far away needs your help and is hoping to hear from you. Take the time to write a letter or make a long-distance call. It will help you both.

Thursday the 4th presents deadlines that are inflexible and getting closer. You can do a lot if you ignore distractions and connect with the focused energy available to you. Exceptional harmony rules in the home. It's a good evening to spend in family activities or to invite special friends to join you for dinner. Relaxing company makes everyone feel like contributing.

Weekly Summary

As the week begins, you will have completed your recovery from the low point you reached last week and will be ready to again take charge of your life with energy and enthusiasm. You are productive, lighthearted and open to the romantic prospects you are likely to enjoy. You focus your attention on the home and get involved in repair projects and remodeling. The only sore point will be the difficulty you have getting ideas across; this may cause friction with your mate.

The weekend may end with a family gathering interrupted by some minor problem with machinery. Communication will be emphasized at the early part of the workweek, and your leadership will be important. You need to concentrate on avoiding your tendency to neglect details. Health considerations will be a factor later in the week, but they won't prevent your interest from turning again to romance.

Amorous pursuits become something of a preoccupation when you need to focus on meaningful projects. Family and work will be your primary concerns by the end of the week, both sources of strength and enjoyment.

45th Week/November 5–11

Friday the 5th you may be called upon to step into a leadership position. You are greatly esteemed by those you work for, and this demonstrates it for all to see. It is a day when challenges are commonplace, but you will rise to the occasion. You have to let go of something you have been holding onto; it has probably outlived it's usefulness. It's a period of change and growth.

Saturday the 6th Aquarius will feel quietly satisfied about recent developments in his or her life. Change is probably the only constant at this point, but this is what opens exciting new horizons for you. Don't let your partner feel left out. There might be some envy that you can deflect with a few well-chosen words. Always include those who are important to you in all aspects.

Sunday the 7th is a good day to sit back and take stock of what you have. Don't succumb to material striving, but remember what is of primary importance to Aquarius. Some of your ideals have been temporarily eclipsed, so a restatement and reinforcement of beliefs is apropos. At the same time, don't be too hard on yourself. Enjoy what fortune has brought you recently.

Monday the 8th is a day to stay away from clandestine manipulation and intrigue. Honesty will yield the best results even though it might initially hurt someone. After a short while, anger will recede, and you can mend broken fences. You probably want to evade certain responsibilities because travel will be necessary and you don't feel ready for it.

Tuesday the 9th will find high spirits at home countered by tension at work. Your supervisor may have some blunt words for you that might deflate you a bit, but the outcome will be positive. New associations in the workplace will generate unexpected benefits in the future. Leave stress behind and optimize the time you have at home. Healthful living should be your priority

Wednesday the 10th brings new business needs that demand new thinking. You are the one to lead the way and help others respond to unfamiliar challenges. You may spend part of the evening working on a political campaign and will likely have dinner with friends. Your active participation in various aspects of life fuels your inner fires and galvanizes your drive to excel.

Thursday the 11th will be difficult because there is a disappointment related to romance. A budding relationship that seemed promising will hit a bump in the road and take an unfortunate detour. It is too soon to give up on this one because all the cards are not yet on the table. Patience here will be your best ally. You may seek out a professional for advice on financial matters that confuse you.

Weekly Summary

The week opens with a challenge that exemplifies the growth and change occurring in your life. You are crossing the threshold into a new stage that will be exciting and offer new opportunities. You must be careful not to neglect those people in your life who are closest to you and not to lose sight of those goals and ideals by which you have chosen to live your life.

Changes will continue throughout the early part of the workweek. You should make an effort to be honest even though it might cause some ruffled feathers. You will soon have your turn to be the recipient of blunt words that will give you pause. You will have a frenetic week but will find that your active life energizes rather than enervates you. You should be able to coast past most difficulties you find blocking your progress.

The end of the week sees its only significant negative note. You will hit a snag that will seem to mean the end of a promising relationship, but don't be too hasty to reach that conclusion. In this case, and to augment this week of change, patience may bring a surprising result.

46th Week/November 12–18

Friday the 12th will be a day of solitary pursuits as you formulate new plans related to family health needs. You will not be troubled by petty irritations, so you can complete this burdensome task. Don't get distracted by your need to let off steam. There will be plenty of time for that later. Spend the evening in an impromptu celebration with a small group of good friends.

Saturday the 13th sees energy at a low ebb, but a traveler from the West may bring news that will perk you up. You need to meet responsibilities related to education, perhaps concerning a course you are taking or a child's progress at school. There might be some wistfulness during the early evening as something you have been looking forward to proves a disappointment.

Sunday the 14th a lost book materializes to provide the answer to a conundrum that has been dogging you for weeks. This paves the way for carefree relaxation that is conducive to romance. It is a good day to go out on a limb and take a risk. If you look inside, you may see what has been holding you back for so long and discover a way to move past it.

Monday the 15th Aquarius will seek protection from the demands of the outside world and want to stay in bed and pull the covers over his head. There is nothing to fear because good fortune is indicated, but there is a strong tendency toward emotional withdrawal. A jolt will come from a work associate that will inspire you to action. Teach children rules of fair play in games.

Tuesday the 16th you feel the need to be with people, but at the same time you send unconscious signals that they should keep away. Your chaotic state derives from being torn between introversion and extroversion and not knowing which way to turn. An animal will be the key to which side of the chasm you really need to be on.

Wednesday the 17th will be a day of totally unfettered imagination. you are very sensitive to outside influences and will again hear the cries of those in need. You will probably make a contribution to a charity and look for other ways you can help. The answer to certain social problems seems quite evident to you, and you may become embroiled in a heated debate with someone who holds a diametrically opposed view.

Thursday the 18th you feel refreshed and have a very active day. A sojourn to a museum or gallery is likely. You will also spend time looking at photos of a colleague's vacation and fantasizing about places you would like to visit. Good relationships will be the norm, and your hectic pace will bring you in contact with people you haven't talked to in recent weeks.

Weekly Summary

Health and financial concerns will occupy much of your attention early in the week. There is some difficulty getting work done in the face of your need to loosen up and relax, but later in the day a pleasant social gathering is indicated. There will be an up-and-down day when good news is countered by a disappointment.

You will wrestle with overcautiousness because there will be a day that is very conducive to risk taking, but your inclination is toward the opposite. It will take a jolt from outside to get you to relax and let good things happen.

There is a day of change when you will be pulled in two different directions and are unable to take a stand. By the time you muddle through this impasse, the week is almost over, and you are ready to enjoy what comes your way. You will be very open and communicative and will want to share some of your material abundance with others who are not quite so lucky. You take advantage of your persuasive skills to try to get others to see things your way. You end the week with creative thoughts racing through your mind and go out of your way in search of additional stimulation.

47th Week/November 19–25

Friday the 19th indicates a need to make some changes and the desire to expend the necessary effort. You aren't looking forward to the weekend because you are committed to a visit you don't want to make. You are stimulated by a project at work that will monopolize your attention for most of the day. There will be a gathering that causes you to get home later than planned, resulting in some friction.

Saturday the 20th you will seek out people to help you maintain the intellectual acuity you perceive to be slipping away. Rather than doing the chores you had planned for the day, you may devote yourself to a creative task related to a hobby. A gift of something you made rather than purchased might not be accepted in the spirit you intended.

Sunday the 21st Aquarius will go on a shopping trip, but someone who had planned to join you will be unable to do so. The impending holiday season seems like a burden when you first contemplate it, but despite yourself, you have to admit that the spirit is winning you over. You get grandiose ideas about entertaining at home, but your partner brings you back to reality with a pungent comment.

Monday the 22nd finds you in a vivacious mood but you succumb to a sense of hopelessness as a host of social ills seems to weigh you down. You feel disappointment that the world doesn't live up to your ideals, but your spirits rise as you remember the blessings it does offer. You may have an opportunity to witness the fruits of your efforts and take great pride in the results.

Tuesday the 23rd Aquarius may meet someone who exerts an intense magnetism for him or her. There will be tantalizing indications that this feeling is mutual, but the time is not right to act on this attraction. In this instance, patience will carry the day even though it means thwarting your yearning for instant gratification.

Wednesday the 24th you will have a full and exciting day leading into the holiday. The pace at work leads to some frustration since you wind up working late, but relaxation comes quickly, and your energy rises throughout the evening hours. You probably should share this with a group as it might be too much for one person to handle.

Thursday the 25th begins with some tension as you are in charge of organizational details and must make sure everything is ready. Your social energy will be strong and you won't allow small upsets to ruin the day. There may be an undercurrent of sadness as you think fondly of someone who is missing from the group. Share the good spirits of this Thanksgiving with loved ones.

Weekly Summary

Creative energy continues to flow in abundance through the early part of the week. You will be less than eager to fulfill some social obligations because you will prefer time alone, capitalizing on the aesthetic focus of your current mind set. You will vainly fight its loss when you finally feel it beginning to slip away, but you know this is probably inevitable.

During the middle of the week you feel enthusiasm for people and begin to get in the spirit of the coming holiday season. This will be short-lived as you will feel some depression at the less than ideal state of the world. Spirits will lift again, partly as a result of the pride you feel when you see the result of earlier efforts.

Getting closer to the holiday, there will be a surge of romantic energy, but patience will be required in order to make the most of it. Your spirits will remain high through the end of the week and the holiday. You spend time with a group of family and friends and this is good since you are bursting with more energy than one person could handle. Your enjoyment of the holiday will be somewhat tempered by the fact that you miss someone who is not with you.

48th Week/November 26–December 2

Friday the 26th. You didn't do it yesterday, so today is the day you are likely to overindulge in food and drink. You can't seem to overcome your fatigue, and rather than do what had been planned, you want to loll about. You will find yourself susceptible to the influence of children which helps get you going. It is a good day to do whatever feels right at the moment.

Saturday the 27th your vitality is again up to snuff, and you will lead others on a whirlwind of practical activity that exhausts everybody but yourself. Housecleaning, painting, shopping, yard work, saving the world are on your agenda. There is no end to the tasks you will address today. Be careful that you aren't insufferable toward those who get in the path of your tornado. Go slowly and remember your health regimen.

Sunday the 28th Aquarius should make an effort to harness the manic energy he or she feels because there is a danger of burnout. Take some quiet time for reflection, reading or romance. It is a good time for communication, so writing letters makes optimum use of the day. If you can slow yourself down, it is also a good time to look to the future and formulate some long-range plans.

Monday the 29th brings the focus back to relationships. Pay attention to people as you are sensitive to their needs and feelings and can make a contribution where it is most needed. You have the ability to create an intense rapport with others and will be able to offer advice that will strike to the heart of their problems. This is a day you can really make a difference.

Tuesday the 30th Aquarius will be impatient with routine and want to ring bells and otherwise shake things up. Sometimes this is good, but be sure your aspirations remain within the realms of reality. You seek change partly because you feel it coming and anticipation has made you anxious to quicken its arrival. Results will be positive but patience is called for.

Wednesday December 1st finds you reflecting on an eventful year that has brought new dimensions to those areas of your life that were lacking. You also contemplate the future and this fills you with ambition and eagerness to do some hard work. Relationships, particularly in the immediate family, are intense because they mirror your thoughtfulness.

Thursday the 2nd involves you in group or committee work, but you are impatient with the pace of the proceedings. Your interpersonal skills are not at their best and you tend to rub people the wrong way. Don't offer your opinion where it is not appreciated and keep quiet if you have nothing constructive to contribute. Try not to bring your troubles home with you.

Weekly Summary

You start the week feeling lazy and self-indulgent but you deserve it because you have worked hard. You should do whatever pleases you at the moment. Your day of rest will restore your energy, and you pledge yourself to saving the world. Communicative abilities will be high, but you have to force yourself to slow down so you can take advantage of them. Some of your zeal should be devoted to formulating more specific plans for the future.

When you finally rest at midweek, you concentrate on affairs at home and make an effort to relate to your mate with a new frankness and honesty. You will be eager to share with compassion and understanding.

Patience will not be your strong suit by the end of the week. You feel overwhelmed by the need to shake things up and rouse the world. At the same time, you will be thoughtful, considerate and not afraid to work hard to ensure a better future. Impatience will cause problems in meetings as the week ends. Don't bring your frustrations home because someone there will need your wisdom.

49th Week/December 3–9

Friday the 3rd Aquarius will still have trouble getting a point across even though you can now grasp complexities and analyze technical problems. Use the day for study and postpone sharing what you learn until another time. Harmony greatly accentuates nonverbal communications; take advantage of this opportunity in an amorous situation.

Saturday the 4th sees things that were troubling you fit neatly into place. Balance reigns among all facets of your personality, and you get along with everyone you encounter. There are items in storage that need to be distributed among family members. It's a good time to make amends and to let bygones be bygones. Issues separating you and relatives can now be addressed.

Sunday the 5th Aquarius will be a magnet for good news; fortune smiles on you from morning until nightfall. Banish all negative feelings, and make new overtures to those who hold grudges and may be angry or distant. Try to break through to a child who has trouble communicating. Today Aquarius is the great peacemaker and is aggressive bringing people together.

Monday the 6th finds you very much in touch with powerful emotions. You are prone to extreme sentimentality and feel very attached to familiar places and objects. At the same time, you should use your inner fortitude to confront those situations that threaten to disrupt the day. Someone at home wants your help, but your self-involvement puts you in danger of overlooking this need.

Tuesday the 7th stretches your patience to the breaking point; you have been working assiduously on a project and the end is still not in sight. You need to forge ahead and keep your final objective in clear view. To ease this ongoing strain, take someone special to dinner. It's a fine evening for romance, recreation and sports. The studious Aquarius will make headway on a research project.

Wednesday the 8th is a good day for shopping. You are generous but not careless and have a keen nose for a bargain. Try not to procrastinate on some distasteful jobs that need to be done before the holidays. Beware of clumsiness as it might lead to an embarrassing situation. Delay physical activities until tomorrow as there is an imbalance between mind and body.

Thursday the 9th favors public relations and sales. Aquarius can readily persuade others to his point of view or sell them anything. You may address a group related to your volunteer activities and will handily win over the crowd. Avoid the tendency to use your glib tongue to manipulate others. This is a time of imbalance between emotional needs and the demands of the outside world.

Weekly Summary

The week begins with an emphasis on insight coupled with a frustrating inability to express what you so readily understand. Nonverbal communication will heighten the intensity of a romantic encounter. Things will continue to fall smoothly into place well into the weekend. Disputes are easily smoothed over and resolved. Good fortune will be with you.

You overflow with sentiment at the beginning of the workweek and are impatient to finish a long-term project. There will be a danger of overlooking someone who is counting on you, so pay attention to the people around you.

An imbalance between mind and body may make you clumsy. You have to force yourself to keep your nose to the grindstone so some distasteful jobs can be completed. Your own emotional needs continue to be at odds with the demands of the world. By the end of the week, your difficulty with articulation will have turned 180 degrees, and you will have a silver tongue that enables you to convince anyone of anything.

50th Week/December 10–16

Friday the 10th is strongly influenced by personal feelings, and it will be almost impossible for you to be objective in your thinking. Examine your unconscious before you jump to conclusions about anyone else.

Don't be quick to blame others for obstacles in your path because this exerts a profound negative aura on interpersonal relations.

Saturday the 11th will begin on a trying note with continued difficulty getting along with others, but this will improve as the day goes on. There is a pronounced danger of overspending, so keep a firm grip on your purse strings. Later your energy will flow with less resistance, and things will enter a more harmonious state, with improvement in the quality of relationships.

Sunday the 12th will be colored by an overriding sense of equanimity. Aquarius is composed and slow to anger. The holiday spirit suffuses you with brotherhood and generosity that makes others appreciate your company. There is also an opportunity to make a creative change in an area of your personal life. Travel will be significant this month, so protect your health.

Monday the 13th Aquarius experiences a strong sense of self-discipline that facilitates remarkable accomplishments. Don't waste this energy on trivialities, but focus it on important issues that need attention. This also enables you to make a new breakthrough in a crucial relationship. It is a day to tie up any loose ends that could trip you up later.

Tuesday the 14th you will feel very social and want to be around congenial people, both at work and at home. You might organize a spur-of-the-moment get-together at your house since your mate shares this feeling. Enrich your life by bringing some of your idealism down to earth and sharing the good things you have. Your generosity is pragmatic today and bears concrete results.

Wednesday the 15th calls for moderation in the zealousness with which you pursue your goals. You may risk losing sight of your innate values in a headlong rush to hit short-term targets. Remember that minor details sometimes have to be ignored. Try to direct your thoughts in a more spiritual direction and forget inconsequential hang-ups.

Thursday the 16th finds holiday cheer infecting the workplace to such an extent that productivity comes to a standstill. It is better to go along with it than fight it; besides, your natural social zest impels you to join the frivolity. Tomorrow is more suited to work so little will be lost. Be sure to take this rampant enthusiasm home with you to share with your significant other.

Weekly Summary

Your thinking is somewhat unclear early in the week because emotions are unsettled and prevent objective thought. Relations will be strained because you will be relatively uncommunicative. This problem will clear up by the middle of the weekend, and your feelings of closeness to others will draw people to you. It's a good time for creative change.

Self-discipline will prevail early in the workweek, making it a very satisfying and productive period. Good feelings continue to influence you, and you may host a gathering of friends that will have some long-term benefits you don't expect.

There will be a preoccupation with minutiae later in the week that threatens to derail your forward motion. You need to force yourself to look ahead, rather than at the ground beneath you, so you can avert this difficulty. You may be somewhat grouchy and alienated from the good spirits surrounding you, and to overcome this, you should yield to the tenor of the moment. As the week ends, make an effort to share the holiday spirit with neighbors as well as close loved ones.

51st Week/December 17–23

Friday the 17th is a day of significant accomplishment. Your energy is focused and there is harmony between thought and intellect. You feel very close to the people at home so try to make the most of it. Even though there might be a lot to do, it is a good night to relax and go out to dinner and take in a movie afterward.

Saturday the 18th will be hectic but it will be filled with activities that bring you closer to family and friends. Take time in the morning to look at finances and make sure everything is under control to preclude overspending and a resultant cash crunch farther down the road. You may have to go out of your way to accommodate a child as a favor to an old friend.

Sunday the 19th is a pleasant day although again it will be very busy because you lend assistance to someone who needs it. There are things you need to do yourself, but you give your time willingly and get satisfaction knowing your help isn't taken for granted. There may be a gathering at an associate's house where business will be discussed and final touches added to a project.

Monday the 20th you will be the spokesperson for a group and the request you make for it will be favorably received. Warm feelings predominate and there is nostalgia for times shared in the past. There is strong harmony between you and your mate and you look toward the future with a sense of closeness and optimism, much stronger than has been felt recently.

Tuesday the 21st finds you with personal projects and errands on your mind that prevent you from being very effective at work. Interruptions get on your nerves and you will be somewhat grouchy. You have a tendency to be a bit overbearing and overprotective of those close to you and they may feel somewhat constricted by your love. Go out and pay a visit to a neighbor.

Wednesday the 22nd you feel in perfect sync with the celebrations you participate in. There may be a surprise gift from a secret admirer. You will be tantalized for a while but will eventually realize who your secret benefactor is. It will cause you to see that person in a new light. Be careful of a tendency toward jealousy that may mar the good spirits of the day and season.

Thursday the 23rd brings sensitivity to the fore to produce a seriousness and depth of thought unusual at this time of year. Relations and encounters with others are more meaningful and are enriched by a compassionate warmth rising from deep within. Tidings from distant family members will be happy, and you will feel intimately connected to all those around you.

Weekly Summary

Early this week you have no trouble finishing those projects that had been troubling you. Your satisfaction will be shared with important people in your life. You will be very busy but will take much pleasure from what you are doing, including a favor for a friend.

In the middle of the week, time will be spent in a leadership role with a group you are working with. The bonds between group members will be particularly strong. You bring this same feeling home and feel an uncommon closeness with your mate. You will both look optimistically toward your future together.

As the week approaches its end, you are finally able to move out from under the burden of those responsibilities that you have felt looming overhead. You feel richly connected with the many people in your life. There also will be some tantalizing romantic possibilities that add an additional element of sizzle to the

236 / DAILY FORECAST—AQUARIUS

way you feel about people. While you enjoy people, you also have the mental sharpness and resourcefulness to make you a master of the situations in which you find yourself.

52nd Week/December 24–31

Friday the 24th you will want to get out of work early, but deadline pressures and a demanding supervisor preclude this. Don't let impatience get the better of you at this point. Success will come so don't let these last minute annoyances ruin the rest of the day and evening. A family gathering will be buoyant with good cheer. As they usually are at the holidays, children will be a source of deep delight.

Saturday the 25th. Merry Christmas! There may be some anxiety related to travel difficulties, but good fortune governs, and the warm spirits of the season will abound. You should forget some old wounds and re-establish familial bonds that had been troubled for far too long. You and yours will make the most of this day and of the family gathering that celebrates it.

Sunday the 26th you will enjoy more seasonal merriment because your mood remains light and harmonious. The home and family are primary in your thoughts, and the residual glow from yesterday adds to your satisfaction. You know it will be difficult to return to the workday world after the holiday, but there is much to do before the New Year's break.

Monday the 27th finds you still immersed in the delights of the season, but there are jobs that need tackling before you go back to work. Don't let your responsibilities stress you out. You have the presence of mind to strike a balance between the demands of your job and those of your family although today it will be difficult at times. Consider cutting back on the time you devote to charitable organizations.

Tuesday the 28th will be a strain because you want to be with your friends and family. You will make a good impression and earn the plaudits of your co-workers from coming through in the clutch despite the distraction of the holidays. Now is the time to relax and enjoy the appreciation you have earned for your dedicated efforts throughout the preceding year.

Wednesday the 29th sees your usual objectivity desert you. You have a propensity to be overcritical of those people you have to work with during the course of the day. It is not a good time for discussions or delicate negotiations, but you may be called upon to enter into them. If they can't be postponed, you will be able to summon the strength to hold your own until your mood improves.

Thursday the 30th Aquarius turns to the home as a place of respite. The stresses of work and the holidays are abandoned with a return to the comforting bosom of the family. Children feel your steadfastness and benefit from your company. There is a willingness to share that will foment a stronger connection with your partner. Time spent together suits your nostalgic mood, as you both recount tales of your youthful pasts.

Friday the 31st Aquarius feels vigorous and ready to leap optimistically into the coming year. It's a great day to finalize plans for the future. Take stock of where you have been and where you are going, and you will like what you see. Despite the impact of the holidays, finances are in a good shape. A positive aura will stay with you well into 1994.

Weekly Summary

The week begins with some frustration despite the high energy and resourcefulness you possess. Don't allow this frustration to spoil what will essentially be a good day. The holiday will be a happy one, with Aquarius basking in the warm glow of familial bonds that are deeply satisfying.

Midweek will see some conflict between work demands and the desire to preserve and maintain the holiday spirit. Although it may seem difficult at times, you will find a happy medium between what you want and what you need to do. There may be some additional work-related stress, but you feel appreciated and proud of what you do.

As you approach the final holiday of the year, you will again regain balance and be able to appreciate the abundance in your life. An objective examination of your life enables you to derive satisfaction from things given, things worked for and things achieved. As you look to the coming year, you feel happy and optimistic that your destiny will continue to bring you the good fortune you have been granted. Happy New Year!

DAILY FORECASTS: NOVEMBER AND DECEMBER 1992

Sunday November 1st The focus of today is sleeping very, very late into the day. After all your partying over the weekend you can't even get out of the bed until after noon. Confront a sibling about their open hostility to your dating partner, and you can put an end to it. Travel should go smoothly as long as you are practical.

Monday the 2nd. You are not at your best today physically. If you feel overtired, try to catch a nap sometime during the day. You will be reviewing your prospects and your career progress up to this point. If things are going well, your self-image is upbeat. If things are not going well, you have only yourself to blame.

Tuesday the 3rd. The root of some office tension is your tendency to be controlling and dogmatic. Your subordinates feel they are being pushed around and not given the respect they deserve. If you spread yourself too thin, you may end up changing social plans around.

Wednesday the 4th. An extravagant urge is making itself felt today in Aquarius households. If you have to return goods purchased by your mate or teenaged child, you will feel embarrassed since it means you aren't as well off as you would like people to think. You are having trouble balancing home and work.

Thursday the 5th. You have the discipline now to break bad habits and to develop healthful ones. Any changes you want to make in terms of personal appearance, such as weight loss or better posture, should be started today. A Sagittarius makes friendly gestures to you.

240 / DAILY FORECAST—AQUARIUS

Friday the 6th. Don't get upset if a Gemini or Aries cancels plans at the last minute. You do not have to spread yourself too thin just to follow the crowd. It would be best if you stay home today and get some projects done around the house. You are tempted to go trip the light fantastic in those new, alluring clothes.

Saturday the 7th. Take a chance with a small amount of money, and the returns could be enormous. This is an excellent weekend to get away from burdensome responsibilities. Travel is in the picture, so choose compatible companions for a trip. A Pisces could make things more complicated than they need to be. This week indicates a long-distance call from a relative.

Sunday the 8th. Go on a day trip to the ocean or the mountains, and you will feel greatly rejuvenated. You are thinking a lot about grown children who have moved away from home. Why don't you call them? Your partner gives you a present, and you wonder why he or she is acting so coyly. Dispel your suspicions and appreciate the gesture.

Monday the 9th. New people give this work week an air of suspense and intrigue. Don't try to be controlling; have some fun with the unknown elements of life. You have lots of good fortune related to finances right now. You could have good luck publishing material you worked on several years ago. This break will ultimately put money in your pocket.

Tuesday the 10th. You are erratic in your thinking, unpredictable in your actions, and sarcastic in your speech. This is infuriating to someone who is trying to get into your good graces. Avoid stimulants or over-the-counter medication unless it is prescribed by a doctor. A minor health crisis arises later. A loved one comes to your rescue.

Wednesday the 11th. Cancellations and upsets are par for the course. Your voice will be heard in defense of the underdog at work or school. You are tempted to pick an argument with a loved one, but sanity prevails at the last moment. A quiet evening enables you to plan for some weekend visitors.

Thursday the 12th. Aquarius is naturally a freedom-loving individual, so you assiduously avoid someone who is demanding a heavy commitment from you. However, it seems there is no way to dodge bill collector. Better pay certain debts in full if you can. This is not a good day to borrow money because you will have a hard time paying it back.

Friday the 13th. Today you may meet an attractive stranger who makes your heart skip a beat. Be friendly to newcomers at work, outgoing on line at the post office or bank. You will have to overcome a tendency to be stubborn, which creates a negative first impression. You feel very sensitive about finances and are apt to react defensively by picking poor investments.

Saturday the 14th. Legal problems will work out to your advantage as long as you are fair and open-minded. Be flexible and drop matters if it seems the most prudent course of action. You want to go shopping this afternoon. Be realistic about what others can do for you. If you are a parent, don't overreact to extreme moodiness in your child; it is just a phase.

Sunday the 15th. Bargains abound at an antiques store that you frequent. No one can squelch your ambitions or your dreams, and you have lots of support on the home front. You now should pamper a loved one who recently lavished attention on you. Your mate or a parent has had an exceptionally trying week, and some hugs and kisses would do their ego a world of good.

242 / DAILY FORECAST—AQUARIUS

Monday the 16th. This is a fabulous time for financial speculation. Now your judgment is keen and your information correct. An older relative calls seeking a Thanksgiving invitation. Don't let this person down; it's bad karma to be unyielding and unforgiving. The workplace is fairly calm for the next few days.

Tuesday the 17th. This is one of those favorable days for returning all of your phone calls and completing all overdue correspondence. The written word will avoid misunderstandings later on. Be sure your messages are promptly delivered. You are a little harsh on a family member who was only trying to help you out.

Wednesday the 18th. Today is an excellent time for a conservative investment. Partnerships and alliances are indicated, most notably with a Libra or Gemini. Aquarius gets along easily with another air sign, so look for this type if you want to team up with someone compatible. You have the mental stamina to take charge.

Thursday the 19th. You and a loved one have an argument about money, and you appear to lose in the face of cold logic. Don't take it out on your mate in petty ways. Consider some counseling to work mutual problems out. You feel very suspicious and mistrustful today, but your fears are unfounded.

Friday the 20th. The exploration of different forms of spiritual practice has tremendous appeal to you. Taking a class in yoga or meditation will open up lots of new opportunities. Group activities tap your creativity. You find it easy to express yourself now to those you trust. Your partner suddenly has lots of physical energy, and you have difficulty keeping up with him or her.

Saturday the 21st. If you are single, you may find romantic opportunities at large social gatherings. This is a favorable time to finish old projects around the house. You may be up in arms over loud music at a neighbor's house during the wee hours of the night. Aquarius is usually too easygoing to say anything.

Sunday the 22nd. You owe a Cancer friend a babysitting favor, but you are trying to avoid paying this debt. You may have some problems related to your telephone service. If you have a date, you could end up bored. Your companion is not your dream lover.

Monday the 23rd. Your judgment is really off today, so it would be wise to avoid any money decisions until tomorrow. Focus on clearing your desk. You feel very empathetic to a neighbor or co-worker who is experiencing romantic melodrama and intrigue. You find yourself drawn to strange people and events.

Tuesday the 24th. Today is an easygoing day. Everything seems to be going well, and your mood is bright and perky. Your restless mind might do well tackling a complicated and detailed subject. Study will be rewarding. Errands keep you on the move and out of the office. Plan holidays now so you don't pay full fares.

Wednesday the 25th. A romance with an Aries or a Scorpio could be heating up. You are getting nervous about Thanksgiving because you have been asked to help out with the meal preparation. Rely on a veteran cook to teach you the drill. Buy a new outfit to take your mind off anxieties.

Thursday the 26th. Happy Thanksgiving! You enjoy observing your family and soaking up the warmth and love. Get actively involved; attend to the details. Children figure prominently in the events of this holiday. You think about expanding your own family. Try to spend some private time with your mate.

244 / DAILY FORECAST—AQUARIUS

Friday the 27th. Mechanical things keep breaking down. It would be a good idea to invest in a complete tool kit and an array of extra batteries to keep on hand in the house. You feel neglected, but don't make heavy demands on your partner, who has a need for and a right to some space. A Taurus friend proves loyal.

Saturday the 28th. The weekend can be hectic and upsetting if house guests linger. Aquarius can charm the intruders out of the house, and they never realize it was your idea to send them packing. You have a hard time doing anything constructive today. The phone keeps ringing, and friends keep stopping by. You complain, but deep down are pleased by the attention.

Sunday the 29th. You find yourself enjoying children more lately. You are very self-conscious about your appearance today. If might not be a bad idea to try a new hairstyle or go for a new look in clothes and shoes. Some of your outfits are outmoded, not even trendily old-fashioned. The offbeat Aquarius will want a public image to match a zany personality.

Monday the 30th. It is very difficult to get things accomplished today since your mind is elsewhere. There is a challenge at work, either a complicated gadget or an intriguing new employee. As usual, you are the first to take on a dare, and so can turn the situation to your advantage. Don't be offended by the chance remarks of a loved one. Wear blue or gold to boost your image.

Tuesday December 1st. A Pisces Moon, beginning this morning, stirs up your emotions and makes you dream the impossible dream. You want to accomplish things you never considered before. It's time to travel down new avenues in life. Take a chance, explore new territory, live life on the edge. At least glance at the possibilities without using artificial substances. Stay upbeat.

DECEMBER—1992 / 245

Wednesday the 2nd. Aquarius may not be able to cope with problems at work because your energy level is low. There are a million minor details that are driving you crazy, and you don't possess the patience or drive to finish projects. You feel inhibited rather than creative. A Pisces friend trying to drag you into a personal drama will drag you down instead of drawing you out.

Thursday the 3rd. You can't seem to get new projects started. An idea emerges, then vanishes as soon as the telephone rings, which it will often today. These are the days prior to an eclipse. It would be prudent to avoid making any important decisions now. It is better to think about things rather than act on them. You feel unsociable, which is unusual for outgoing Aquarius.

Friday the 4th. If you are going through a bad patch with a lover, try to see things from his or her perspective. It seems as though everyone is coping with tumultuous personal problems, so you should not feel alone. You are opinionated and stubborn about an issue in the office or with a neighbor. Try to be more tolerant.

Saturday the 5th. A friend could introduce you to someone who is incredibly attractive to you. However, you should wait until after the eclipse ends on the 13th before you make any moves toward this person. He or she could be concealing some disturbing secrets. Given a chance to judge, you might not make a favorable decision. Get out and have fun on the social scene.

Sunday the 6th. This is not a good day to travel, but it is an excellent time to make travel plans. Consult loved ones before you draw up an itinerary. Your mate's agenda may conflict with yours today, so you will go out to meet new people. Get your work done in the morning. A Capricorn who puts you down while demanding your best is just testing your limits.

246 / DAILY FORECAST—AQUARIUS

Monday the 7th. Personal goals seem to be at a standstill, but your career is rolling right along. You feel impatient with the pace at work, but the slowdown is just a passing phase. Things are bubbling behind the scenes, which bodes well for you in the long run. Make a special dinner for a partner who needs loving attention. Avoid traveling today and tonight if you can.

Tuesday the 8th. Your judgment is not too good most of the day. Avoid scheduling any interviews or doctors' appointments, since things will go wrong at the last minute. Financially, you are in good shape, but don't get overconfident about how much you can spend personally. Be up for a social event.

Wednesday the 9th. You cannot count on the help or affection of your loved one, and relationships with your closest friends will be unstable. The source of the difficulty could be money. It may be better to work at home today; you could get more done. Your moods are up and down, but try to go with the flow.

Thursday the 10th. If a friend appears to be breaking things off, you have a fair-weather friend. Deception rules now, so a separation may be temporary. You should be alert for exploitativeness. Some people are using you for monetary gain. You are very sensitive about yourself, and will go to any lengths to prove yourself to newcomers. This tendency could make you a loser. Be a loner instead.

Friday the 11th. Your romantic life, though interesting, has not been as spine-tingling as you would like it to be. The lack of excitement will go on a while, but patience is a virtue. There has been no shortage of suitors; but no one of them has taken your breath away lately. Don't worry, soon someone will sweep you away. There is some help at work from influential people.

Saturday the 12th. If you are a partnered Aquarius, your relationship is having its share of ups and downs. Things start to get better now. Try to be flexible and understanding, which is easy for the mature Water Bearer who knows the value of compromise. Both you and your mate are preoccupied with work and family.

Sunday the 13th. The Moon in Leo makes you foolishly generous today, inclining you to buy more gifts than common sense would dictate. Everything you've purchased so far is thoughtful and appropriate, so stop there. An issue with your partner dominates your thoughts during the day. Get out of the house tonight and socialize. It will make you feel better.

Monday the 14th. If you have been feeling neglected by your friends, talk to them about it. You may find they have been feeling the same way. The office environment is uptight right now. You meet a Sagittarius who does something funny, and it really makes your day. If you are working on a budget, get your figures right. Be methodical, and do not ignore any details.

Tuesday the 15th. If you feel amorous, invite someone special out and see what happens. If you lack energy, you may benefit from a fitness course that involves outdoor exercises. A health club can provide a balanced program. At home, you might try weights or an indoor bicycle. Relax more and enjoy your family. Phone a brother or sister, which will lift their spirits.

Wednesday the 16th. Someone wants to have their way with you, but you are not interested. Don't avoid something that could be fabulous under a different light. Focus on the friendship factor and diplomatically disregard the physical. Cultivate your mind by taking night classes. You have a healthy intellectual curiosity now. Catch up on your reading.

248 / DAILY FORECAST—AQUARIUS

Thursday the 17th. You are excited and distracted by the swirl of holiday happenings. Make advance plans for a romantic tryst with the significant other in your life. No one can argue with reservations made and paid for, even an independent type you choose as your new lover. Something you thought was lost turns up. You don't have a lot of physical energy so don't push it.

Friday the 18th. Aquarius may be too free making speeches and sounding off in general. You will hurt someone's feelings by talking behind their back. You want to tell everyone your opinion, but they don't want to hear it. You have a keen interest in a Leo or Sagittarius. Make an obvious move, or this person will not know you are interested.

Saturday the 19th. Aquarius is losing points with some friends now. You deeply offend someone without even realizing it. Yet it is another friend who sits down and tells you about it. This is a good day to get a lot of errands done, especially in the morning. Your instincts are correct regarding a money matter. Someone in high office noticed your work and is ready to reward you.

Sunday the 20th. You have the barest minimum of concentration at work. You also have little patience for people who don't make much effort to get things done right the first time. Just bear with it, and don't lose your temper with co-workers. Arguing makes you look silly. You have excellent rapport with a child, who needs some discipline. Buy yourself a treat today.

Monday the 21st. A Cancer intrigues you now. This person is probably too moody, sensitive, and family-oriented for the easygoing Water Bearer. But you are swept up in the traditional holiday spirit, so you connect. Don't work late; your partner needs someone to talk to. A business partner has good financial advice.

Tuesday the 22nd. There is no time to coddle a spoiled person in the work environment. You have been feeling a bit under the weather, so it might be a good idea to take a day off to pamper yourself. Get someone else to pamper you. Double-check with family members to make sure holiday plans are going smoothly.

Wednesday the 23rd. The press of deadlines keeps you busy during business hours, as there is a lot left to do before you and colleagues close up shop. Then there will be the holiday preparations. You have a chance to chat with family members you haven't seen for some time, and at one point you are moved to tears. Your partner is especially loving and attentive.

Thursday the 24th. An eclipse will heighten excitement and anticipation of surprises. You are quite likely to learn all sorts of new and interesting things about friends and family members. A honeymoon, perhaps an elopement, is indicated for some Aquarius. Wherever you are, you will be in a sharing mood, ready to celebrate or pray with the people around you.

Friday the 25th. Merry Christmas! Despite a general aura of unpredictability, goodwill and hope dominate this holiday. People are not behaving the way they normally do, which could be problematic for some. Dinner holds some surprises. Aquarius will be assessing future prospects and making some tough decisions. Don't let a relative's snide comments affect you.

Saturday the 26th. A relative confesses a secret to you about something that happened a long time ago. While returning a Christmas present, you meet a charming Aries with whom you went to high school. Even if your partner is unavailable, there is no reason not to go out tonight and have some fun. Don't get too excited about a new car; you can't afford it right now.

250 / DAILY FORECAST—AQUARIUS

Sunday the 27th. A cousin, niece, or nephew does something charming, and out of impulse you buy him or her an expensive gift. A friend's chance comment gives you some insight into yourself. There is a lot of post-holiday cleanup that must be done. Ask those who shared the fun for help. Don't let anyone take advantage of your good nature.

Monday the 28th. Don't avoid responsibilities at business. There is some paperwork that needs to be done, so get to it even if you are not in the mood for busy work. Your relatives can be helpful in making some financial decisions. When you balance your checkbook, you realize that tight budgeting will be needed.

Tuesday the 29th. You need to be honest with people and tell them exactly what you think in order to set a positive tone for future business prospects. This tack is surprisingly successful, as people appreciate your frankness. This is a good time to look at property or other real estate investments. Do not overanalyze a partner's odd behavior. Go with your intuition.

Wednesday the 30th. Be careful around mechanical devices and electrical appliances. Don't get involved in an argument between two relatives. Avoid alcohol and drugs. Mind- and mood-altering substances can be dangerous; they might make you do something you would regret, in addition to making you feel physically bad. A hobby or study project is a cure for the blues.

Thursday the 31st. It's New Year's Eve, and you are out of control. Rather than celebrate, although you might do plenty of that, Aquarius is focused on the need to make more money. You have so much energy and enthusiasm now, with an Aries Moon spurring you on, that your dreams probably will come true. Meanwhile, enjoy your evening by the time 1993 arrives.

Most Accurate Astrologer Since Nostradamus!

SHE CAN 'SEE' 30 YEARS INTO THE FUTURE—AS FAR AS THE YEAR 2022!

As Hailed on Cable and Network Television!

Yes! You've Seen Her on TV and Been Amazed by Her Incredible Predictions Such as These:

LIKE: 5 of the 6 winning numbers in the giant 52-million FL State lottery held in Oct. '88...all 6 winning numbers in the Feb. '89 PA lottery

LIKE: All 3 of the Love Disasters that brought down Jim Bakker, Jimmy Swaggert & Donald Trump.

NOW, SPEAK TO HER DIRECTLY HEAR HER PREDICTIONS FOR YOU
(YOUR LUCKY NUMBERS, LUCKY DAYS, LUCKY SIGNS)

Not For Her Usual $300 Fee...But FOR JUST THE PRICE OF A PHONE CALL
—and not a single penny more!

NINA AND HER ENTIRE FAMILY HAVE 'SEEN' THE FUTURE FOR OVER SIX CENTURIES!

Just A Few Of The Incredible Predictions By The House Of Nostradamus That Came True:
- Lincoln's Death
- 'Frisco' Earthquake
- 29' Stock Market Crash
- Assassination of JFK
- Death of Elvis Presley

Small wonder that the Nostradamus family power to see the future has been sought after by personalities and organizations as: The President and Mrs. Ronald W. Reagan, L.A. Dodgers baseball team, numerous State Police Departments across the nation.

Imagine picking up your phone...and hearing your future as told to you by the head of the greatest family of seers...THE HOUSE OF NOSTRADAMUS.

Your own lucky days and numbers...'up periods' when you should reap your fortune...Plus, 'down days' when you should avoid major decisions.

AND ITS ALL YOURS... NOT FOR THE $300 IT WOULD USUALLY COST YOU FOR A PERSONAL, ANALYSIS BY MADAME NOSTRADAMUS—but for just the price of a call.

CALL NINA DIRECT:
1-900-370-9014
LOTTERY NUMBERS FOR YOUR STATE

Do you need help with a problem? Want to multiply your chances of winning the lottery? The answers are a phone call away!

Why is Madame Nina Nostradamus willing to offer you this prediction analysis not for her usual $300 fee—in fact, without you sending a single cent? Because she is convinced that after your first call... when you hear her predictions and see them come true...you will become one of her regular clients and gladly pay her $300 fee for your personal analysis.

1-900-420-9005
PERSONAL HOROSCOPE PREDICTIONS

Only 2.99/min. Hold That Call, NYC.

Here's What You Get When You Call Nina:
- Your personal lucky days and numbers
- 2 predictions relating to job, finance
- 3 predictions about love & relationships
- Lottery & sweepstakes picks in your State

NOTES

First, Give Me Your Birthday, Then—
PICK 3 CARDS and I'LL GIVE YOU YOUR FUTURE FOR THE NEXT 3 MONTHS

AMAZING TRIAL OFFER

In Each of These Vital Areas of Your Life:
- LOVE •MONEY •HEALTH •LUCK •JOB •BUSINESS
- UPCOMING GOOD & BAD DAYS •NEW RELATIONSHIPS

Plus
Lucky Numbers for Winning the Lottery!

Madame Zorina Zoltan, tarot-card reader for the rich & famous, predicts your future—call her direct NOW!

YOU ARE NOW LOOKING AT THE TAROT CARDS OF FATIMA
The Most Accurate Predictors of Your Destiny!

#01	#02	#03	#04	#05	#06
World	Temp.	Lovers	Priest	Fool	Tower

#07	#08	#09	#10	#11	#12
Death	Moon	Strength	Justice	Devil	Magic

PROVEN 98.7% ACCURATE! CALL HER TODAY and HEAR WHAT DESTINY HOLDS FOR YOU!

Do you need help with a problem? Would you like to know your destiny for the next 3 months—TODAY? The answer is only a phone call away...and for this one-time-only trial offer...not for Zorina Zoltan's usual $300 consultation fee...but your FOR JUST THE PRICE OF A PHONE CALL—AND NOT A SINGLE PENNY MORE!

LIKE HAVING A CRYSTAL BALL THAT SEES 3 MONTHS INTO THE FUTURE

Be amazed as Zorina Zoltan reveals to you:
- Your future in love, money, relationships, career and health
- Your lucky days & numbers for 3 months
- 'Up' periods to take advantage of and 'Down Days' to beware of
- Even how the Tarots of Fatima can multiply your chances of winning the lottery by 700%!

TO HEAR YOUR FUTURE FOR THE NEXT 3 MONTHS—

1. Call Zorina Zoltan and give her your birthday.
2. Next, give her your own pick of any 3 Tarot cards pictured above.
3. Zorina will analyze your picks, then predict your future in all vital areas.

For Personal Tarot Reading
1-900-370-3313

For Your Lucky Lottery Numbers
1-900-370-3314

Only $2.99/min.

Hold That Call, NYC. Must be 18. Touch-tone phones only.

NOTES

New Phone Service Now Available to Public!

SHE WILL CAST ONE OF HER 7 PROVEN SPELLS FOR YOU!

Just as She's Done for Over 1,000 of the World's Richest & Most Famous People

Meet Countess Maria-Madonna...caster of spells for three U.S. Presidents, jet-set millionaires and 100 movie stars. NOW, HAVE HER CAST A SPELL FOR YOU!

JUST CALL, SEND NO MONEY!

Yes! Receive the Power to Make Others Obey Your Every Command!

PROBLEMS OF LOVE? RELATIONSHIPS? MONEY? CAREER? HEALTH? SHE GIVES YOU TOTAL CONTROL TO CHANGE YOUR DESINY!

Yes! Her psychic spells radiate a force so potent she can help you earn, win or inherit huge financial gains—enjoy extra years of youthful vigor—recapture a lost love—or even come into a windfall like winning the sweepstakes or hitting the lottery!

NOW! CHANGE YOUR LIFE WITH A PHONE CALL!

Her psychic spells are legendary. So awesome...she can make one person love another...breathe fires of passion into any relationship ...re-unite lovers...solve ALL money problems...overcome sickness...bring years of good luck! INSTANTLY CHANGE YOUR ENTIRE FUTURE LIFE!

HERE ARE THE 7 PROVEN SPELLS YOU CAN CHOOSE:

- SPELL OF WISDOM & SUCCESS—for job, business, school
- SPELL OF FAME & GLORY—for success in show business, athletics, public careers
- SPELL OF RICHES—for life-long luxury
- SPELL OF BLISSFUL LOVE—to bring people closer together
- SPELL OF UNUSUAL GOOD LUCK—to win lottery, track, Vegas or Atlantic City
- SPELL OF PROLONGED LIFE—for years of youthful vigor and zest
- SPELL OF POWER & VICTORY—to overcome rivals and defeat your enemies

not for her usual fee of $500— **BUT FOR JUST THE PRICE OF A PHONE CALL** *and not a single penny more!*

SPECIAL LUCKY SPELL OF THE FULL MOON

...to make any 6 numbers and any 5 days you choose extra lucky for you in lottery, bingo, cards and track...CALL:

1-900-370-3312

Only $2.99/min.

HERE'S ALL YOU DO:

1. SEND NO MONEY. Just call, that's all.
2. Choose 1 of the 7 spells above and tell the Countess to cast it for you immediately.
3. Be amazed when within 24 hours YOUR MIRACLE WISH begins to come true!

To Have a Spell Cast for You, Call:
1-900-370-3310

Hold That Call, NYC. Must be 18.

Are You Destined For True Love?

America's Leading Psychics and Astrologers Are Finally Available To Tell You!

The most accurate psychics in the nation were previously available only to the rich and powerful. Now you can consult with them on your own phone! Discover your secret destiny. Ask about marriage, money, success and happiness. Call now and talk LIVE with your own personal psychic. Call Now!

The Beverly Hills Psychic Center

CALL 1-900-680-2324

$2.95 Per Minute 24 Hours
Sponsored by Telecom USA
P.O. Box 487, Wallingford, PA
19086